TEACHER'S GUIDE

Lifting
AS WE CLIMB

Effective Bible Study Lessons

WILL SMITH

Teacher's Guide
LIFTING AS WE CLIMB
by Will Smith

Copyright © 2018, 2020 William Smith

All rights reserved. Except as permitted under U.S. Copyright Act of 1976, no part of this publication may be reproduced, distributed, or transmitted in any form or by any means, orstored in a database or retrieval system, without the prior written permission of the publisher.

Published by: Lifting As We Climb
Visit our website at www.givingbiblestudies.com

Library of Congress Cataloging-in-Publication Data: filed

ISBN-13 978-0-9857429-2-8

Printed in the United States of America

Introduction to the Bible Study Teacher's Guide

A Must Read For The Bible Study Teacher!!!

Greetings Bible Study Teacher,

Thank you for purchasing this Teacher's Guide and the Student Workbook; it's a 20 lesson Bible study journey. It's my goal that you will see your purchase as an investment in eternity.

The answers to each lesson are given for your convenience. Your guide and the Student's Workbook has supplements for lessons 2, 5, 8, 9, 10, 11, 14, and 16. The supplements are given to help your student to better understand a question in the lesson or in some cases to better understand the lesson itself. The Teacher's Guide will show you when and where the supplements will be needed.

Before I put this Teacher's Guide into one book and the Student's Workbook into one book, I would give the student one lesson per session and the supplement was given at the time of the question in the lesson or during the lesson.

Because the supplements and the lessons are together in one book, your student may be tempted to glance at future lessons. I discouraged it in the introduction to the Student's Workbook. So, hopefully they won't glance ahead. If they do, they probably won't understand what they see and read. Please discourage your Bible study student from looking at upcoming lessons. Here is exactly what I said to them in the introduction:

"In your hands is the entire 20 lesson journey called, *Lifting As We Climb*. You will be tempted to glance ahead at future lessons. But please, please, resist that temptation and focus on the current lesson your Bible teacher is on with you. If you glance ahead at future lessons, you may want to ask your Bible teacher questions about those lessons. And it would be premature for your Bible teacher to answer questions on future lessons because each lesson builds up to the next lesson. And also, if they answer questions regarding future lessons, they would cheat you with their answers because the answers will be given more fully when you get to that lesson. And I don't want you to get confused by looking at future lessons."

Soul-winner, may God bless you as you share the hidden treasures in the Word of God. And it is my prayer that your student accepts Christ as their personal Lord and Saviour and get baptized.

If you have any questions, you can always email at will@givingbiblestudies.com , info@givingbiblestudies.com , or fill out the contact form if you're on the website.

Peace and love,
Will Smith
The Author

Understanding The Bible
Lesson 1

1. Who wrote the Bible? 2 Peter 1:21
   Holy men as they were inspired by the Holy Spirit. God did not write the Bible, the Holy Spirit inspired men to write it. Men did not use their own thoughts to write the Bible. God wrote three times in the Bible: The Ten Commandments- Exodus 31:18; the handwriting on the wall- Daniel 5:22-28; Jesus wrote on the ground- John 8:1-11.

2. What is the purpose of the Bible? Psalm 119:105; 119:9-11; 2 Timothy 3:16; Hebrews 4:12
   Psalm 119:105 – The Bible is a spiritual flashlight or guide to light up our path on earth and to lead us to heaven. Without the spiritual flashlight we would stumble in the spiritual darkness like most people in this country and the world.
   Psalm 119:9-11 – Study of the Bible keeps the young and old out of sin.
   2 Timothy 3:16 – The Bible is good for correction and reproving us when we're wrong.
   Hebrews 4:12 – The Bible is like a two-edged sword, it cuts deep. The Bible not only judge our acts but it judges our motives.

3. Why should I study God's Word for myself? Acts 17:10,11; 2 Timothy 2:15
   Acts 17:10,11 – We should study God's Word for ourselves so that we may know the Word of God for ourselves and not depend on people (pastors, Bible teachers, etc.) for biblical understanding.
   2 Timothy 2:15 – Study of the Bible gets God's approval and it helps us so we won't be ashamed of not knowing the Word.

4. How can I greatly benefit from studying the Bible? Isaiah 28:9,10
   Early in the chapter, the priests had become drunkards so God said that He has to teach them when they are babes.
   "Precept upon precept, precept upon precept; line upon line, line upon line." A precept is a doctrine. We must compare Scripture with Scripture. When we compare, one verse can bring more understanding then the previous verse. Like this lesson on the Bible, a verse in Peter showed us who wrote the Bible but the verse in Peter could not help with the purpose of the Bible. We had to go to Psalms and other verses. Martin Luther and the Protestant Reformers said, "Scripture interprets Scripture." It teaches us to be **responsible Bible students** and not build a belief system on one verse.

5. What does Jesus say about the Bible? Matthew 4:4; John 5:39; Luke 24:27,44
   Matthew 4:4 – He said we should not live by bread alone but by the Word of God.
   John 5:39 – Jesus says the Bible talks about Him. Amen!
   Luke 24:27,44 – Jesus showed these two disciples where the entire Old Testament talks about Himself. Wow! Jesus giving a Bible study. What was that like? He pointed to the sacrifices, the Feast Days, etc. and how all of it pointed to Him, the Messiah.

6. How does Job value the Word of God? Job 23:12
   To Job, the Word of God was more important than his daily food. We should read at least a few verses of the Bible and meditate upon them (but not limit our study to a few verses) each day to get spiritual strength and to find out what God's will is for us today.

7. What is God's ultimate desire for me in studying the Bible? John 20:31; Romans 15:4
   John 20:31 – That We receive Jesus as our personal Lord and Saviour!!!
   Romans 15:4 – That we might have hope; many are losing hope today because there are so many depressions which at times lead to suicides.

Do you understand that the Bible is God's inspired word?

Is it your desire to know and understand more about Jesus?

The Origin of Sin
Lesson 2

1. What is sin? 1 John 3:4
   Sin is breaking any of the God's Ten Commandments.

2. Where was the first war and who were the participants? Revelation 12:7-9
   There was a war in heaven? Yes, the first war was in heaven. How would you describe heaven before reading about a war being there? Heaven can be described as beautiful, peaceful, serene, safe, holy, and loving and the list goes on.

3. How many angels were cast out of heaven with the devil? Revelation 12:4; 1:20
   Revelation 12:4 – one third of the stars were cast out.
   Revelation 1:20 – the stars, in Revelation, are symbolic of angels.

4. Who is Michael?
   See Supplement 2-A.

5. How does the Bible describe Lucifer before and after his fall into sin? Ezekiel 28:13-17; Isaiah 14:12-14

   Lucifer before his fall:
   - The covering cherub – he was in God's presence with his wings surrounding God;
   - Beautiful
   - In Eden
   - Perfect

   Lucifer after his fall:
   - Conceded- heart lifted up because of his beauty
   - Proud; see Proverbs 6:16-19 to see how much God hates pride above all other sins
   - One reason God hates pride is because pride brought Lucifer down to be a devil and pride brought Adam and Eve down to be sinners (Genesis 3:3)

6. What is temptation and what is God's role in it? 1 Corinthians 10:13; James 1:13
   1 Corinthians 10:13- God does not give us more temptation than we can handle.
   James 1:13- God does not tempt us. **See Supplement 2-B.**

7. Who causes sickness, death, and disaster? Job 1:6-19; 2:1-7; Ephesians 2:1,2
   Job 1:6-19; 2:1-7 – The devil is behind it all.
   Ephesians 2:1,2 – The devil is called the prince of the power of the air. The devil is behind terrible storms, earthquakes, hurricanes, and tornadoes. He wants to kill people en masse. What a huge mistake when insurance companies call these disasters "an act of God."

8. Whose child am I when I disobey God? Acts 13:9,10
   The child of the devil

9. What is the devil's aim here on earth? I Peter 5:8
   To kill us. The devil wants sinners dead so they won't accept Christ as their personal Lord and Saviour. And the devil wants Christians dead so they can stop telling people about Christ.

10. Why is the devil so hateful today? Revelation 12:12
    He knows his time is short. The devil reads the Bible to see what God is up to and the devil understand the signs that will take place before Jesus comes.

11. How can I overcome Satan and his temptations? James 4:7; Ephesians 6:11-18
    James 4:7 – Give yourself to God.
    Ephesians 6:11-18 – Putting on the whole armor of God, spiritually speaking the amour means:
    - taking time to pray
    - study the Bible before leaving the house

    This gives us the spiritual strength to handle crazy stuff at work and school. Instead of the devil's "fiery darts" (vs. 16) affecting us negatively, they will bounce off of us the way bullets and knives bounce off of the Bat Mobile when there is danger.

12. What will ultimately happen to the devil? Ezekiel 28:18,19
    He will turn to ashes

Do you understand what sin is and how it began?

Is it your desire to resist the devil and his temptations?

Michael—The Archangel
Lesson 2-A

I. Meaning of the terms Michael and Archangel

    a. Michael – taken from the Hebrew word "Mika'el" which means "One who is like God"; Michael is Jesus (see text below).

    b. Archangel – taken from the Greek word "Archaggelos" which means "high" or "chief" angel.

II. Identity of Michael the Archangel

    a. **Revelation 12:7-9** – In these verses Michael and his angels are fighting with Satan and his angels.

    b. **Jude 9** – Here Michael, the Archangel, is contending with Satan over the body of Moses.

    c. **Daniel 10:13,21** – In these verses Michael comes to help Gabriel. Gabriel has the highest position of the created angels (**Luke 1:19**). The only position greater than this is that of Jesus, the Holy Ghost or God the Father; yet Michael comes to Gabriel's aid.

    d. **I Thessalonians 4:16** – In this verse the Archangel's voice is heard accompanied by the trump of God and "the dead in Christ rise."
    John 5:25-29 – These verses identify whose voice is heard that wakes up the dead saints; Jesus says in **vss. 28,29** "…all that are in the graves shall hear His voice and shall come forth…" Jesus' voice is heard thus making Him the Archangel. This same context is used in **Daniel 12:1,2** where it speaks of Michael standing up and the dead come up out of their graves.

Temptation
Lesson 2-B

THE MEANING OF TEMPTATION
To represent an evil as a good; an enticement to sin. Sin in its true nature is ugly, brutal, and destructive. In the hour of temptation sin is seen as fun, pleasurable, exciting, rewarding, or maturing —anything but its true nature.

Temptation is not sin. The tempted need not accuse themselves of guilt in their being liable to temptation. Sin only begins when we yield to temptation. Satan tempts with the intention of causing defeat. God does not tempt us nor does He allow more temptation than we can handle

—**James 1:13; I Corinthians 10:13**

Five Steps to Christ
Lesson 3

1. **FAITH**
    a. What is faith? Hebrews 11:1
        Faith is complete trust in God even when you have no evidence God is going to do what He says. Faith is belief that God will save me. Faith is belief that God can save me. And faith is belief that God is in the process of saving me. "Wait, God is in the process of saving me even if I have not yet accepted Christ as my Lord and Saviour? Yes, He got you to the point of saying yes to the Bible study, so His saving process for you has begun.

    b. How can I please God? Hebrews 11:6
        By having faith in Him; if there is no faith, we cannot please God; John 20:26-29- Faith believes without seeing.

2. **REPENTANCE**
    a. What is repentance? 2 Corinthians 7:9,10
        Repentance means 'change'. It's a change of heart; remorse for sin; an awakening of our mind as to just how sinful we are. And repentance means a turning away from sin and turning to God. The turning away from sin may not take place right away but the person no long wants to continue to live in sin; it may be an attitude change but the real change is coming. On Sabbath, at the end of the sermon, the pastor makes an appeal or an altar call for people to come forward to accept Christ as their Saviour or to receive Bible studies. When a person responds to the altar call, they are experiencing repentance. They want to change something in their lives. The changes may or may not occur that day but most changes do take place during the Bible study sessions.

    b. How does repentance happen? John 16:13
        The Holy Spirit. We cannot do it on our own. The Holy Spirit prompts any right impulse in us. Whether it is a desire to do right, a desire to pray, to study the Bible, to go to church, He is the One who prompts us to do it (John 16:7,8; Philippians 2:13).

    c. Why do I need repentance? Psalm 51:5; 58:3; Jeremiah 17:9
        Psalm 51:5 – We were born in sin. We have a slant or bent towards evil that is incurable with Jesus. That's why we need the Holy Spirit to lead us to repentance. In theology, the term "original sin" refers to the sinful nature Adam and Eve passed on to their children on down to our parents passing that nature on to us. That's why we have some of our fathers and mothers evil traits of character.

Sorry, even if they are saints of God, they cannot pass on their righteous traits of character, only the evil.

Psalm 58:3 – We are born liars; it is not a learned behavior.

Jeremiah 17:9 – Our conduct is dreadful. The last clause, "who can know it?" Do you know that you have no clue as to how evil you can be? Remember when in the heat of anger you said or did something to someone and less than ten seconds later you wish you had not said it or done it? You didn't know just how evil you were. Thank God that He subdues some of the evil in our hearts so we don't end up killing somebody and ten seconds later apologize.

    d. Is everyone guilty of sin and what is the result of sin? Romans 3:23; 6:23
Romans 3:23 – Yes, everyone is guilty of sin
Romans 6:23 – The result of sin is death but thank God for Jesus who died for us.

3. CONFESSION

    a. When will God forgive me of my sins? 1 John 1:9
When we confess our sins. God not only forgives but He cleanses us from sin

    b. What are two conditions of having my sins forgiven? Psalm 51:3; Matthew 11:28-30
Psalm 51:3 – We must acknowledge or admit to our sins and that we are a sinner. Just like in Alcoholics Anonymous, first timers must admit or acknowledge they are alcoholics or exit the program.
Matthew 11:28-30 – We must be willing to give our sins to Jesus; the load is too heavy for us to bear. We tell close friends and family members things we don't tell anyone else but we know they can't always help us. But at least we get the stuff off of our chest. With Jesus though, He can help us.

    c. What happens if I don't confess my sins? Proverbs 28:13
God will not forgive us if we don't confess.

    d. What does it mean to have my sins forgiven by God? Romans 3:24,25
Instant acquittal. God no longer sees our past sins but, at the moment of confession, He sees us as spotless. And He sees us as if we were always spotless. Have mercy! Thank You Father!

4. CONVERSION

    a. How does Jesus explain conversion? John 3:1-8
Being born again. A new spiritual life has taken place.

    b. How can I get saved? Ephesians 2:8,9; John 3:16
Ephesians 2:8,9 – By the grace of God; grace is an unmerited or unearned favor

from God. We don't deserve it nor will we ever deserve it. We must exercise faith to receive God's saving grace.

John 3:16- God sent Jesus to die for us because God and Jesus and the Holy Spirit loves us.

   c. What happens when I am born again? 2 Corinthians 5:17; 1 Peter 2:1,2

2 Corinthians 5:17 – All things become new. Just as your newborn son, daughter, brother, sister, nephew or niece has new eyes, new ears, new feet, etc., so does a newborn Christian. The newborn Christian has new eyes and don't look at the same evil shows or evil movies; new ears and don't listen to filthy music; new feet and don't go to night clubs and unchristian parties. If a person professes to be born again and they are still doing the same things before their profession, that are not born again. (**Note: Bible Instructor**, now is a good time to give or repeat your testimony especially the part on how you became new).

5. **OBEDIENCE**
   a. What will I love to do after I am saved? John 14:15; 1 John 3:22

John 14:15 – We will love to keep God's Ten Commandments. Spouses are faithful to the marriage vow because they love each other not because someone is making them do it. We obey God's Ten Commandments because that is our response to His love for us.

1 John 3:22 – We seek to please God.

   b. Did Jesus obey His Father's commandments? John 15:10

Yes, and Jesus is our Example (1 Peter 2:21).

   c. What is Jesus waiting for me to do? Revelation 3:20

Open the door of our hearts to Him. Jesus will not force His way into our hearts. In Holman Hunt's masterpiece of Christ standing on the outside knocking on the door, he's sending a powerful message. The door represents our heart. But there's something unique about the door; there's no doorknob on the outer door. Jesus can only enter our heart if we let Him in.

   d. How should I live after Jesus has entered my heart? 2 Corinthians 5:15; Galatians 2:20

2 Corinthians 5:15 – We should live differently from before we let Jesus come into our hearts. A definite change must take place. We should live for God and no longer for ourselves. When I was a teenager my parents told me to guard my actions and to not bring reproach upon the Smith name. When we become Christians, God does not want us to bring reproach upon the name of Christ.

Galatians 2:20 – How can we know for sure if we have been born again? You'll know when the things you loved (drinking, drugs, premarital sex, etc.), you begin to hate and the things you hated (church, Christians, reading the Bible, etc.), you begin to love. And you'll know when God takes away the love of sin, the habit of sin, and the desire to sin. Medical doctors may be able to help us with the second, the habit. They tell folks that if you keep drinking you will die from cirrhosis of the liver; when told that the habit disappears. But only God can help us with the other two. He can take away the love of sin and the desire to sin. How do I know? God did it for me. And "the life I now live in the flesh I live by the faith of the Son of God, who loved me, and gave Himself for me."

Do you understand the FIVE STEPS TO CHRIST?
Have you already accepted Jesus as your personal Lord and Saviour?
Do you desire to accept Jesus as your personal Lord and Saviour? (If they say yes, you can lead them to accept Christ as their personal Lord and Saviour; see below).

Father, I know I am a sinner and I ask that you forgive me of all my sins (name some). I have no power to quit doing these things. Thank You for sending Jesus to die on the cross for me. I want Jesus to come into my heart as my personal Lord and Saviour. And please give me the Holy Spirit that I may be able to live for Thee. Father, thank You for forgiving me of my sins, in Jesus name I pray, Amen.

Note: After your Bible student prays the above prayer, they may feel lighter because the burden of sin has been lifted. But no lightning will flash. We're saved by faith, not by outward displays. Let them know that their sinful record in heaven has been erased. They are clean now!

The Second Coming of Christ
Lesson 4

1. What promise is made to me as I look for Jesus? Hebrews 9:28
    Jesus will come again the second time and save us. Note: when the verse says, "without sin," it is referring to Jesus not dying on the cross again because He did it once (see Hebrews 7:22-27). So please be assured, "without sin" does not mean or imply that Jesus sinned when He was on earth (see John 8:46; 2 Corinthians 5:21).

2. What is the purpose of this grand event? John 14:1-3
    For Jesus to be reunited with us. He has been physically away from us for almost 2,000 years and now it's a grand reunion. Think of the joy you have when you see loved ones you have not seen in years.

3. How will Jesus come? Acts 1:9-11
    He will come as He left, in a cloud. The disciples saw Him leave and we will see Him come back.

4. Will only the Christians see Jesus when He returns? Revelation 1:7; Matthew 26:57, 62-64
    Revelation 1:7 – No.
    Matthew 26:57, 62-64 – There will be a special resurrection for those who pierced Him; those responsible for putting Him on the cross.
    For the Secret Rapture Theory, see the book, *Lifting As We Climb*, pp. 74-76.

5. What noise will resound and who will rise first at the Second Coming?
    1 Thessalonians 4:16,17
    What will be heard is the voice of the Archangel and a trumpet blast from heaven.

6. What fierce element in nature is the Second Coming likened unto? Matthew 24:27
    Lightning.

7. How does the Psalmist picture my Lord's return? Psalm 50:3
    He says God will not keep silent and winds will be blowing and fire.

8. Who will accompany Christ as He crashes through the sky at His coming? Matthew 25:31
    Christ is coming in His own glory and in the glory of the Father (Matthew 16:27) and all of the holy angels will come with Him. This will produce brightness in the sky brighter than the noon day sun.

9. How do lost folks respond to Jesus' appearing? Revelation 6:14-17
    They run to the rocks and to the mountains and beg them to fall on them. They do this because they lied to family members and friends about coming to church. Now the overwhelming guilt is crushing them and they want a mountain to fall on them rather than look into the face of Jesus.

10. What else happens to the wicked as they look up at Jesus?
    2 Thessalonians 2:8; 1 Corinthians 15:51-55
    2 Thessalonians 2:8 – The wicked are destroyed by the brightness of Jesus' appearing (see question 8).
    1 Corinthians 15:51-55 – The righteous have to be changed instantly to endure the brightness. And, again, since the wicked are unchanged, they are destroyed by the brightness.

11. What am I to do as I anxiously await my Master? Matthew 24:44; Luke 21:34-36
    Matthew 24:44 – Be ready.
    Luke 21:34-36 – Watch for the signs (lesson 5) and pray.

Do you believe and understand that Jesus is coming again?

Is it your desire to be ready when He comes?

Signs of the Times
Lesson 5

1. What did the disciples ask Jesus concerning the end of the world? Matthew 24:3
   The disciples wanted to know when the end of the world was coming. It's interesting that they asked Jesus that question. At the end of Matthew 23, Jesus talked about the end of Jerusalem (vs. 38). The disciples thought the end of Jerusalem meant the end of the world. They thought, "How could the world go on and Jerusalem be destroyed?" So, in Matthew 24, Jesus gave signs that pointed to the end of Jerusalem that was destroyed in AD 70 and signs that would take place at the end of the world.

2. What did Jesus say about the gospel and the end of the world? Matthew 24:14
   Jesus will not come until the world has been warned. God never sends judgment until the people have been warned. The gospel work is not finished anywhere until it is finished everywhere. Three important signs:

3. What are some of the **POLITICAL** and **NATURAL** signs that will take place before Jesus comes? Matthew 24:6,7
   1989 – The Soviet Union broke up. Now independent nations can say yes or no to Christian missionaries.
   1990 – The Berlin Wall that separated West and East Germany was broken up. Now West Germany can invite Christian missionaries.
   1993 – Apartheid in South Africa broken up and now Christian missionaries can go in.

   The signs I give gets out of date and new ones pop up all the time. Give some political (America at war) and natural signs like earthquakes, hurricanes, floods, tornadoes, etc. **See Supplement 5-A, B**. (give up to date statistics when you think it's time).

4. What are some of the **MORAL** signs? 2 Timothy 3:1-5; Matthew 24:12; Luke 21:25,26
   2 Timothy 3:1-5 – Most of these verses are clear. "Incontinent" means without self-control. "Heady" is being quick tempered. "High-minded" is being drunk with pride, with the heart lifted up against man and God.
   Matthew 24:12 – **See Supplement 5-C**.
   Luke 21:25,26 – Men are getting more and more fearful and perplexed because they don't understand what's about to take place—Jesus is coming!!!

5. The Bible says in Daniel 12:4 that at **"the time of the end...knowledge will be increased."** How has knowledge increased over the last 100 years in the area of Technology, Medical, and Travel?

    Give examples in these fields. Just a word though: Pharaoh and his army used horses as they chased the Israelites; that was about 4,000 years ago. Up until Henry Ford invented the automobile, horses were basically our only means of land transportation. So, for almost 4,000 years horses were our transportation. Then within the last 100 or so years, all kinds of inventions came. And the verse says in the last days knowledge will increase. We've been living in the last days for at least 100 years.

6. How does our day compare to the days of Noah and Lot? Luke 17:26-32

    We, too, are so busy that the coming of Jesus is not in our thoughts. Evil prevails and even more evil will emerge. The angel told Lot and his family not to look back and his wife looked back and was turned to a pillar of salt. Her heart was in Sodom.

7. What are the **CELESTIAL (in the sky)** signs and the events under the sixth seal? Matthew 24:29,30; Revelation 6:12-14

    See Supplement 5-D. These events happened already. Look closely at these events. The fallen stars in Revelation 6:13 took place in 1833. Verse 14 it refers to the Second Coming of Christ. We have been living in between vs. 13 and vs. 14 for 185 years (if you're in year 2018).

8. How close does Jesus say His coming is once these signs appear and who knows the day of His coming? Matthew 24:33,36

    Jesus' coming is very near, even at the doors. Only the Father knows the day and hour of Jesus' coming. No man knows despite the fact that man keeps coming up with dates and failing.

9. What is God's desire, as we get closer to the end? 1 Timothy 2:3,4; 2 Peter 3:9

    1 Timothy 2:3,4 – God would love for all people to be saved and to know the truth of His Word.
    2 Peter 3:9 – God would love for all people to repent and to be saved when Jesus comes.

Are you convinced that we are living at the END OF TIME?

Would you be ready if Jesus were to come RIGHT NOW?

Coronavirus (Covid-19) 2020
Lesson 5-A

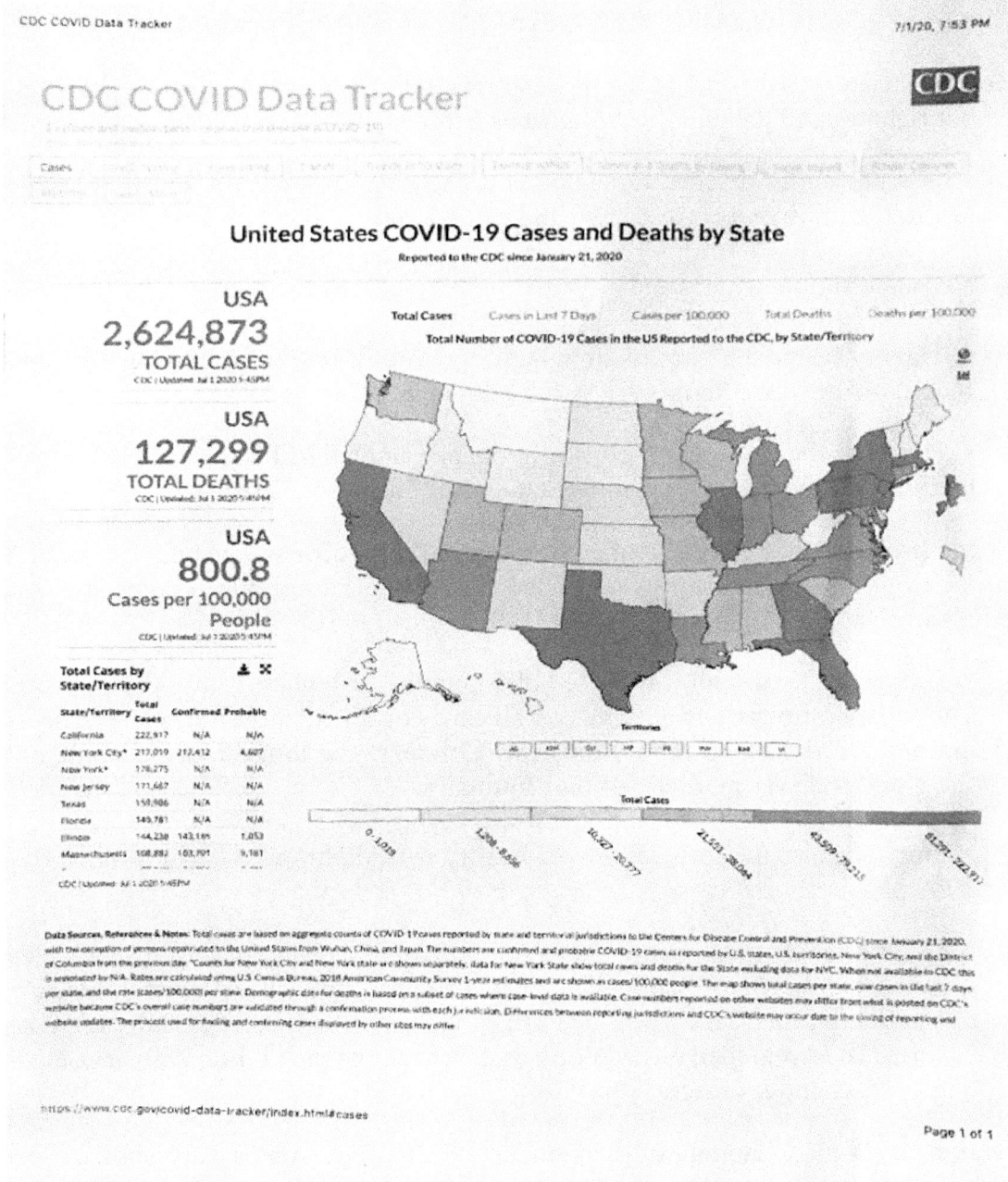

Monster Hurricanes in 2017
Lesson 5-B

AccuWeather Hurricane Expert Dan Kottlowski reported:

Hurricane Harvey was the first of the three storms, developing on August 17, 2017. Harvey started out right around the middle of August as a tropical storm east of the Lesser Antilles.

- It made landfall in southern Texas as a Category 4 storm. The storm moved inland just to the north of Corpus Christi and caused massive flooding in Houston.

- The maximum wind speed of Hurricane Harvey was 130 mph.

- **Harvey lasted 117 hours after making landfall in Texas, beating the previous record** of Hurricane Fern that lasted 54 hours in 1971.

- Harvey is the first Category 4 storm to make landfall in Texas since Hurricane Carla in 1961 and the first in the United States since Hurricane Charley in 2004.

Hurricane Irma became a tropical storm on August 30, 2017. Irma came off the coast of Africa as a strong tropical wave and slowly intensified from a tropical storm to become an extremely powerful storm.

- Irma had a maximum wind speed of 185 mph, the highest of all storms this season. The second strongest max winds of all time for an Atlantic hurricane. **The storm maintained these 185-mph winds for 37 hours, the longest any cyclone around the globe has ever maintained that intensity.**

- Irma was also the first Category 5 hurricane in the tropical Atlantic since Hugo in 1989.

- Irma's strength took a tremendous toll on Barbuda, Saint Barthélemy, Saint Martin, Anguilla and the Virgin Islands. The storm continued to move westward causing major damage in the Turks and Caicos and brushing the northern coast of Cuba as a Category 5 storm. The storm then turned north and went across the Florida Keys, causing major damage and power outages.

Hurricane Maria made landfall on September 20, 2017 and was a very similar storm to Hurricane Irma. Both storms developed from a tropical wave that came off the coast of Africa. But in contrast, Maria did not intensify to Category 5 until it reached the Lesser Antilles.

- Maria caused major damage to the island of Dominica and to Puerto Rico.

"Maria will go down in history as one of the worst storms, if not the worst storm, to ever hit Puerto Rico," Kottlowski said.

Iniquity Shall Abound
Lesson 5-C

JESUS SAID THAT IN THE LAST DAYS, "BECAUSE INIQUITY [SIN] SHALL ABOUND, THE LOVE OF MANY SHALL WAX [BECOME] COLD."—MATTHEW 24:12. AND PAUL SAID, "THE LOVE OF MONEY IS THE ROOT OF ALL EVIL." —I TIMOTHY 6:10.

Several years ago, James Patterson and Peter Kim published the results of a national survey on morals in *The Day America Told the Truth*. They shared some of the things people said they would do for money. Here are some of the things people said they would be willing to do for $10 million (along with the percentage of people who would do it). They would…

- Abandon their entire family (25 percent)

- Become prostitutes for a week or more (23 percent)

- Give up their American citizenship (16 percent)

- Leave their spouse (16 percent)

- Withhold testimony, letting a murderer go free (10 percent)

- Kill a stranger (7 percent)

- Put their children up for adoption (3 percent)

James Patterson and Peter Kim, *The Day America Told the Truth: What People Really Believe About Everything that Really Matters.*

"These are the times that try men's souls."
Lesson 5-D

GREAT EARTHQUAKE – NOVEMBER 1, 1755
"By far the most spectacular earthquake of earlier times was that of Lisbon, in 1755. This has some claim to be regarded as the greatest earthquake on record. If it is possible to believe reports, the felt area, was certainly more than 700 miles in radius.

"In 1755, the damage to Lisbon itself was very great. At that time, the city had about 230,000 inhabitants, nearly 30,000 of whom were killed, according to conservative estimates." —G. A. Eiby, *About Earthquakes*, New York: Harper, 1957, pp. 141,142.

SUN DARKENED – MAY 19, 1780
"The 19th of May, 1780, was a remarkable dark day. Candles were lighted in many houses; the birds were silent and disappeared, and the fowls retired to roost. The legislature of Connecticut was then in session at Hartford. A very general opinion prevailed, that the Day of Judgment was at hand. The House of Representatives, being unable to transact their business, adjourned. A proposal to adjourn the Council was under consideration. When the opinion of Colonel Davenport was asked, he answered, 'I am against an adjournment. The day of judgment is either approaching, or it is not. If it is not, there is no cause for an adjournment: if it is, I choose to be found doing my duty. I wish therefore that candles may be brought.'" —Timothy Dwight, *Connecticut Historical Collections*, 2nd ed.; New Haven: Durrie & Peck and J. W. Barber, 1836, p. 403.

"Sudden darkness appeared around 10'o clock in the morning, so dark that you couldn't read a newspaper outside, it lasted until midnight of the next night." —*Noah Webster's Dictionary*, 1869 Edition.

MOON BECAME AS BLOOD – MAY 20, 1780
"In connection with this extraordinary phenomenon [sun darkened], the moon was reported to appear red...the exact cause has never settled."—*Independent Chronicle* [Boston], May 25, 1780.

STARS FALL FROM HEAVEN – NOVEMBER 13, 1833
"I witnessed this gorgeous spectacle and was awe-struck. The air seemed filled with bright descending messengers from the sky...I was not without the suggestion that it might be the harbinger of the coming of the Son of Man...I read that the 'stars shall fall from heaven', and they were now falling...I was looking away to heaven for the rest denied me on earth."
—*Life & Times of Frederick Douglas*, Pathway Press (original ed.,1855) p.117

The Millenniium
Lesson 6

The word millennium is not in the Bible. It's a Latin word that means one thousand years (mille-1,000; annus-year). The 1,000 years referred to in this lesson is only found in Revelation 20. The Bible mentions 1,000 years in other places but it does not have anything to do with the 1,000 years mentioned in Revelation.

READ REVELATION 20:1-9 BEFORE DOING THE LESSON:
This lesson is the only one that is not in question form. It's in three parts.

I. **Events which mark the <u>beginning</u> of the Millennium**

1. Jesus comes the second time. John 14:1-3
   Does Jesus' coming start the millennium or could it have already started? Could we be in year 487, 253, or 891 of the millennium? We are in year 17 of a millennium so could the millennium have started already? No, the millennium did not begin yet. In Revelation 20:3 it says that when the millennium starts the devil "should not deceive the nations no more, till the thousand years should be fulfilled…" Is the devil deceiving nations now? Yes! Then the millennium has not started yet. When will there be a time when the devil cannot deceive the nations? When Jesus comes he will not be able to deceive. The righteous living and the righteous dead will be in heaven. The wicked living will be destroyed by Jesus' brightness (lesson 4) and the wicked dead will remain dead (Revelation 20:5). That's how we know the Second Coming of Jesus begins the millennium.

2. The righteous dead and the righteous living are taken to heaven. I Thessalonians 4:16, 17; Revelation 20:6
   See note on #1

3. Jesus' brightness destroys the wicked living. II Thessalonians 2:8
   See note on #1

4. Satan is bound and cannot deceive people. Revelation 20:1-3
   What binds Satan is the fact that he cannot deceive. He has been deceiving for at least 6,000 years of earth's history and who knows how long he was deceiving the angels in heaven. All is his deceiving is brought to a screeching halt when Jesus comes.

II. **Events that occur <u>during</u> the Millennium**

1. The wicked dead remain dead. Revelation 20:5
   Since the wicked were destroyed by the brightness at Christ's Second Coming, they remain dead during the Millennium.

2. The earth is desolate and looks like a vast wilderness. Revelation 20:2; Jeremiah 4:23-27
   Like a sci-fi movie. It's dark and everyone is dead lying on the ground and smoke begins to ascend from the ground, then the closing credits appear out of nowhere.

3. The saints are involved in a work of judgment with Jesus. Revelation 20:4; 1 Corinthians 6:3; Revelation 15:1-4
   Revelation 20:4 – This judgment is not about who will go to hell; that has already been determined. The righteous are in heaven so it's not about them. It's not about the righteous determining the degree of punishment for the wicked. God will determine that. This judgment has to do with fairness. Other than a family member or close friend, who do you really believe is going to heaven? Picture the person in your mind. If, when you get to heaven, and you do not see the person in heaven you can ask Jesus or an angel what happened. You will be directed to the person's book. There you will find the dark side or secret sins that caused the person to be lost. The books are there for us to see that God was fair in His judgment of the lost person.
   1 Corinthians 6:3 – Saints will judge fallen angels.
   Revelation 15:1-4 – How can the righteous sing "Just and true are Thy ways…" if we don't know God was just. We can see it for ourselves in the books. And in verse 4 it says, God's "judgments are made manifest" by the books.

III. Events at the <u>close</u> of the Millennium

1. The wicked dead are resurrected. Revelation 20:5
   Having been destroyed by the brightness at the Second Coming of Christ, and remaining dead during the Millennium, the wicked first time waking up is at the end of the Millennium.

2. The devil is loosened and goes out to deceive the wicked. Revelation 20:7,8
   Note: What loosens the devil is that he has people to deceive. Remember, what bound him was he had no one to deceive.

3. The holy city descends upon the earth. Revelation 21:1,2
   The holy city in heaven with its golden streets and the righteous people within comes down to earth at the end of the Millennium.

4. The devil and the wicked attack the holy city and fire comes down from God out of heaven and devours them. Revelation 20:9; 21:18

   It's dark and the only light is in the distance, the holy city. The devil convinces the host of the wicked to attack the holy city. Included in the wicked, are kings, queens, doctors, lawyers, pastors, CEO's, PhD's, rich folks, and poor forks. With the devil, all bring their skills to the table as to how to destroy the city. The righteous people, on the inside of the city, can see outside of the city and all of the activity going on. In fact, the righteous may see their sons, daughters, brothers, sisters, mothers, and fathers they prayed for but the loved ones never said yes to Jesus and present truth. Then the righteous sees it; something they never ever wanted to see. They see fire come down from God and kill the wicked. This is hell's fire and the final end of the devil, sin, sinners, and death.

5. God cleanses the earth by fire and creates a new earth wherein dwells righteousness and sin shall not rise up the second time! 2 Peter 3:10-13; Nahum 1:9; Isaiah 65:21

    2 Peter 3:10-13 – God cleanses the world by fire and recreates a world where righteousness dwells.

    Nahum 1:9 – Affliction will not rise the second time. God will not tolerate sin ever again. Sin ran its course for some 6,000 years but never again.

    Isaiah 65:21 – Once God recreates the earth, the righteous will live the holy city and go out and build houses and vineyards. God will resume what He intended for Adam and Eve. And the righteous will live happily ever after!!! AMEN!!!

Is it your desire to be on the inside of the holy city looking out, or on the outside looking in?

What Happens When A Person Dies
Lesson 7

1. Does a person have a soul? Genesis 2:7
   No, a person is a soul. Look at the verse. Man did not receive a soul, he became a soul.

2. What two elements make up a soul? Genesis 2:7
   The two elements are the dust of the ground and the breath of life.

3. What happens to the breath of life and the body at death? Ecclesiastes 12:7
   The spirit (the breath of life) goes back to God and the dust (body) returns to the ground, we bury folks when they die. Some Christians believe the spirit and the soul are the same; they are not. At death, the soul no longer exists because you need breath and body for the soul to exist.

4. Does a person have an "immortal soul?" Job 4:17
   No. All people are mortal. Mortal means can die and immortal means cannot die.

5. Who only has immortality? 1 Timothy 6:14-16
   God the Father, Jesus and the Holy Spirit.
   The teaching of Natural Immortality and the Immortality of the Soul in man is not biblical.

6. How and when do Christians receive immortality? Romans 2:6,7; 1 Corinthians 15:51-55
   How? Romans 2:6,7 – In verse 6, Paul says one way we receive immortality is by well doing (being righteous). And in verse7, he says we seek immortality which means we don't have it yet.
   When? 1 Corinthians 15:51-55 – Paul says we receive immortality when Jesus comes the second time which means we don't have it yet.

7. Where do the wicked and the righteous go at death? Job 21:30-32 (wicked); Acts 2:29,34 (righteous)
   Job 21:30-32 – The wicked go the grave at death, not to hell.
   Acts 2:29, 34 – The righteous go to the grave at death, not to heaven.

8. Can dead people think? Psalm 146:3,4; Ecclesiastes 9:5,6,10
   No.

9. Can dead people haunt those who are living? Job 7:9,10
   No.

10. Who then are those individuals that resemble our deceased relatives and friends? Revelation 16:14; 1 Samuel 28:3, 5-15; 2 Corinthians 11:14,15.
    Revelation 16:14 – The spirits of devils working miracles.
    1 Samuel 28:3, 5-15 – The first seance is the Holy Bible where a live person attempts to talk to a dead person. This is what happens when folks pay money to see palm readers.
    2 Corinthians 11:14, 15 – The devil and the fallen angels (demons) have the power to transform themselves to look and sound like our deceased loved ones and friends.

11. When will the righteous dead come out of their graves? 1 Thessalonians 4:16, 17 – When Jesus comes and not a moment before.

Is it clear to you that both the righteous and the wicked dead are PRESENTLY in their graves?

The Fate of the Wicked
Lesson 8

1. Was "hell" prepared for people? Matthew 25:41
   No, hell was prepared for the devil and the fallen angels (demons, imps). Man will end up in hell because of his disobedience but it was not prepared for man.

2. Does the "everlasting fire" that Jesus spoke of in question 1 mean eternal torment? Malachi 4:1-3; Ezekiel 28:13-19
   No, the everlasting fire Jesus spoke of off above does not mean eternal because all the wicked will turn to ashes including the devil, the first and worst sinner (Ezekiel 28:19 lesson 2).

3. What does Jude 7 mean when he says that Sodom and Gomorrah suffered "the vengeance of eternal fire?" 2 Peter 2:6
   2 Peter 2:6 says those cities turned to ashes. And those cities are not burning today. An eternal fire is a fire that cannot be put out by man. It's a fire that God ignites and it does not go out until everything turn to ashes. And the results of the fire is eternal, not the suffering. The fire department in Sodom was on fire and they could not put that out nor could they help the people.

4. What is meant in Revelation 20:10 by the term, "tormented day and night for ever and ever?" 1 Samuel 1:22, 28 (Psalm 30:12; Acts 2:29,34)
   1 Samuel 1:22, 28 – Hannah, Samuel's mother, said that after Samuel be weaned (stop breast feeding) he was going to turn him over to Eli the priest and Samuel will abide with God forever. Then in verse 28 she says that Samuel will be with God as long as he lives.
   Psalm 30:12 – David says, he will sing praises to God and give Him thanks forever. Then in Acts 2:29, 34 (lesson 7), Peter says David is dead and buried. What's going on in these verses? The stories tell us that Samuel will abide with God forever then it says as long as he lives and that David will give thanks to God forever and then we learn that David is dead and buried. The point is that forever, in the Bible outside of referring to eternal life, has a beginning point and an end point; it's temporary. People in the Old Testament and the New Testament understood this. So when John, in Revelation 20:10, says that the devil and the wicked will be tormented day and night forever and ever, the people understood that they will burn until they die, no life in them. And as Malachi 4:3 puts it they will burn until they turn to ashes. No unending torture for the wicked; God is love and cruelty is Satanic.

5. Read the story in Luke 16:19-31. Is it a literal story or a parable?
It's a parable. It cannot be literal because people in heaven cannot talk with those in heaven (lesson 6). Jesus said the righteous and the wicked receive their reward when He comes back not at death as told in the story (lesson 4). And the body goes to the grave at death not to heaven or hell (lesson 7). **See Supplement 8-A**

Is it clear to you that a person who goes to hell does not burn for eternity?

The Everlasting Dwelling Place of the Soul
Lesson 8-A

As soon as the sentence is given, the soul is snatched away and hurried to that place which is to be its home for ever and ever! Crowds of hideous devils have met together. With cries of spiteful joy they receive the soul…Immediately the soul is thrust by the devils into prison which is to be its dwelling-place for ever more. The prison of each soul is different, according to its sins.

The Third Dungeon–THE RED HOT FLOOR

Look into this room. What a dreadful place it is! The roof is red hot; the walls are red hot; the floor is like a thick sheet of red hot iron. See, on the middle of the red hot floor stands a girl. She looks about sixteen years old. Her feet are bare, she has neither shoes nor stockings on her feet; her bare feet stand on the red hot burning floor. The door of this room has never been opened before since she first set her feet on the red hot floor. Now she sees that the door is opening. She rushes forward. Listen, she speaks! She says, "I have been standing with my bare feet on this red hot floor for years. Day and night my only standing place has been this red hot floor. Sleep never came on me for a moment, that I might forget this horrible burning floor. Look at my burnt and bleeding feet. Let me go off this burning floor for one moment, only one single, short moment. Oh, that in the endless eternity of years, I might forget the pain only for one single moment." The devil answers her question. "Do you ask," he says, "for one moment to forget your pain. No, not for one single moment during the never-ending eternity of years shall you ever leave this red hot floor!" —J. Furniss, *Tracts for Spiritual Reading*. New York: P.J. Kennedy, Excelsior Catholic Publishing House, 1882, pp. 12, 19.

Healthful Living
Lesson 9

1. How does God want me to honor my body? I Corinthians 10:31
   Glorify him in what I eat or drink or whatever I do. Paul emphasized eating and drinking because that's where man fell.

2. What were the first foods God allowed us to eat? Genesis 1:29
   Fruits, nuts, and grains.

3. What food was added after our sin? Genesis 3:18
   Herbs of the field or vegetables. After Adam and Eve sinned, God saw his body beginning to decay so God added vegetables for the iron and minerals.

4. What flesh foods did God allow us to eat after the Flood? Leviticus 11:1-7 (animals); 9,10 (seafood); 13-20 (fowls/birds) (see Deuteronomy 14 for additional foods)
   See Supplement 9-A.

5. What will happen to those who are found eating swine (pig/hog) and other forbidden animals when Jesus comes? Isaiah 66 15-17
   They will be destroyed. If you need more help, see Food Objection Section in book, *Lifting As We Climb*.

6. What does the Bible say about wine and strong drink? Proverbs 20:1; 23:29-35.
   It's not good for us. **See Supplements 9-B-C.**

7. How should I regard cigarette smoking, drugs, and other drinks (coffee, tea, etc.) that are not caffeine free? I Corinthians 3:16,17
   We should not use them. **See Supplement 9-D.**

Do you desire to give up these forbidden things in God's word?

Do you want Jesus to help you where you are weak?

Healthful Living
Lesson 9-A

The following food list was taken from **LEVITICUS 11 (DEUTERONOMY 14)** and **PROVERBS 20:1; 23:29-35**. Always remember **I CORINTHIANS 10:31; 3:16, 17**.

THINGS THAT CAN BE USED FOR FOOD (CLEAN FOODS)- LIST DOES NOT INCLUDE EVERYTHING JUST <u>MOST</u> THINGS PEOPLE CONSUME:

MEATS	FISH	SHORTENINGS	DRINKS
Chicken	Perch	Any vegetable, olive, canola, or peanut oils	Fruit drinks
Beef	Whiting		Soft drinks
Turkey	Trout		White milk
Lamb	Tilapia		Herbal teas
Goat	Salmon		Any drinks
Deer	Tuna		<u>without</u>
	Flounder		caffeine
	Snapper		
	Bass		
	Spot		

THINGS THAT CANNOT BE USED FOR FOOD (UNCLEAN FOODS)- LIST DOES NOT INCLUDE EVERYTHING JUST <u>MOST</u> THINGS PEOPLE CONSUME:

MEATS	FISH	SHORTENINGS	DRINKS
Hog/Pig	Crabs	Hog lard or animal fat;	Coffee
Rabbit	Lobsters	Read ingredients to avoid	Teas or soft
Raccoon	Catfish	**LARD**	drinks with
Possum	Shrimp		caffeine
Squirrel	Oysters		Wine
Turtle	Clams		Beer
Snails	Crayfish		Gin
Horse	Whale		Vodka
Snake	Scallops *(in the clam/oyster family)*		Whiskey
	Mussels		

One report showed that 1 in 6 pigs were infected with the "trichina worm" from which comes the disease—**TRICHINOSIS**.

Shrimp feed on the material on the ocean floor; some eat the parasites from the gills and scales of fish; groups of fish gather near these shrimp waiting such cleaning.

Prohibition Brings Peace to Alaska Town
Lesson 9-B

The devastating social aspects of alcohol use were forcefully demonstrated in the village of Barrow, Alaska. In 1994, they voted to ban the sale and use of alcohol. Many locals [people] up to that time were not able to work because of drunkenness. A top police official said that before the ban, "There was mayhem and tragedy everywhere." Rape, suicide, and drunk and disorderly conduct were rampant. Fetal alcohol syndrome rates skyrocketed. However, abrupt changes took place almost immediately after the ban went into effect, as the following statistics indicate:

- The 3,900 people in Barrow, Alaska voted to ban the sale and use the alcohol in 1994.
- Alcohol-related crime and accidents plunged. Crime fell 70 percent during the one year period of prohibition.
- Regarding acute health problems: Emergency room alcohol-related visits dropped from 118 per month to 23 per month in the first 30 days of prohibition.

McCoy C. The Wall Street Journal. November 15, 1995.

A year later this happened…

"A vote in favor of lifting the yearlong alcohol prohibition in Barrow, Alaska, has been certified.

"The Barrow City Council voted, 4 to 2 to certify the election, which favored alcohol possession by 910 to 834."—- Associated Press, October 13, 1995.

The Effects of Alcohol on the Body
Lesson 9-C

In every state in the United States, it's illegal to drive with a Blood Alcohol Concentration (BAC) of **0.08 percent**. The degree and extent of mental impairment is related to the blood-alcohol level. Studies indicate that definite impairments begin at about **0.03 percent**, which is achieved simply by drinking a 12-ounce can of beer or 5 ½ ounces of ordinary wine by an average 150-pound person. At **0.05 percent** alcohol [about two drinks of 12 ounces of beer]… the peripheral (side) vision drops 18 degrees and depth perception 74 percent. —Rolla N. Harger, "The Response of the Body to Different Concentrations of Alcohol: Chemical Tests for Intoxication," 1964.

By one drink is meant the ingestion of the following amounts of the respective beverages which supply an equal percentage of alcohol to a person's body:

ONE DRINK
1 ½ ounces of whiskey
3 ½ ounces of fortified wine
5 ½ ounces of ordinary wine
12 ounces of beer

As stated earlier, one drink generally causes **0.03 percent** alcohol in the blood of an average 150-pound person. Two drinks double the percentage. Kenny and Leaton report that at a **0.05 blood-alcohol level**, "the 'newer' parts of the brain, those controlling judgment, have been affected." This becomes apparent, since a person "may become loud, boisterous, making passes; saying and doing things he might usually censure. These are the effects that mistakenly cause people to think of alcohol as a stimulant." —Jean Kinney and Gwen Leaton, *Loosening the Grip. A Handbook of Alcohol Information*, 1983.

Yet, it's okay to drink and drive with up to **0.08 percent blood alcohol level**. No wonder the statistics below are so staggering; folks are driving impaired and crashing and killing themselves and others long before they hit **0.08 percent**, the illegal limit, let alone those who exceed the legal limit.

In the United States:
90,000 people die yearly from drinking (60K men; 30K women).

11,000 people die yearly from drinking and driving (30% of all driving deaths).

Alcohol kills more teenagers than all other drugs combined.

Almost $100 Billion is spent annually to purchase alcohol.

Over $115 Billion is annually for the cost of damage to society from alcohol (divorce courts, health care, lost work, premature deaths, etc.).

Note how Proverbs 23:29-35 relates to the above statement:
29 Who hath woe? who hath sorrow? who hath contentions? who hath babbling? who hath wounds without cause? who hath redness of eyes?
30 They that tarry long at the wine; they that go to seek mixed wine.
31 Look not thou upon the wine when it is red, when it giveth his colour in the cup, when it moveth itself aright.
32 At the last it biteth like a serpent, and stingeth like an adder.
33 Thine eyes shall behold strange women, and thine heart shall utter perverse things.
34 Yea, thou shalt be as he that lieth down in the midst of the sea, or as he that lieth upon the top of a mast.
35 They have stricken me, shalt thou say, and I was not sick; they have beaten me, and I felt it not: when shall I awake? I will seek it yet again.

Caffeine-Supplement
Lesson 9-D

Caffeine is a potent stimulant that affects your brain and autonomic nervous system. It is an illusionary drug that leads you to believe that you feel energetic and are no longer tired while at the same time your body needs rest to re-group in order to function right. Because caffeine gives you a feeling of exhilaration or "pick-up", the commercial companies capitalize on this effect and add caffeine to many of their foods and drinks.

POPULAR DRINKS

BEVERAGES	MEASURE	CAFFEINE CONSUMTION (in milligrams)
Coffee	1 cup	100-150
Tea	1 cup	75-125
Diet Pepsi	12 oz	58.8
Mountain Dew	12 oz	54
Coca Cola	12 oz	52.2
Pepsi Cola	12 oz	38
Sunkist Orange	12 oz	36

"There are serious concerns in the psychiatric literature about caffeine's role in 'unbalancing' the mind. Caffeine has been linked to anxiety, anxiety neurosis, psychosis (a state where a person loses touch with reality), and schizophrenia, the so-called 'split personality' disorder."—*The Effects of Caffeine on Psychological Functioning*, Moxon S. Edelmann RJ.

SEVEN WAYS CAFFEINE IMPAIRS THE BRAIN

Tends to produce dependence
Can cause drug withdrawal reactions
Can cause or worsen psychiatric illness
Impairs physical and mental performance
Can cause toxicity (toxins in the body), and even death
May exert effects that impact on spiritual and social dimensions of our character
Interferes with sleep. Caffeine consumed within an hour of bedtime makes it harder to fall asleep, decreases the total amount of time slept, and significantly worsens sleep quality. Specifically, caffeine decreases the deepest, most restorative stages of sleep (stages 3 and 4). —P. W. Curatolo and D. Robertson, *Annals of Internal Medicine*, pp. 641-653 (The Health Consequences of Caffeine).

The Bible Sabbath
Lesson 10

1. Which day did John say that he was, "in the spirit?" Revelation 1:10
   He was in the spirit on the Lord's day.

2. Which day is the Lord's Day? Matthew 12:8; Isaiah 58:13
   The Sabbath is the Lord's Day.

3. What day of the week is the Sabbath? Exodus 20:8-11
   The seventh day of the week or Saturday. **See Supplement 10-A**. Note: God said, "the" seventh day is the Sabbath. "The" is a definite article referring to something specific. God did not say, "a" seventh day which could mean any seventh day. For instance, Monday is "a" seventh day from last Monday. It's just not "the" seventh day.

4. When did the Sabbath originate and what three things did God do on this day? Genesis 2:1-3
   The Sabbath originated or began the first seventh day of the Creation Week. The three things God did on the seventh day were: He rested, He blessed the day, and He sanctified the day meaning God made it holy (God's presence makes the Sabbath day holy or His presence makes anything holy, the sanctuary, the Holy Bible, etc.). He made the seventh day holy for a special use, for us to worship Him.

5. What belief systems or teachings would not exist if all 7 plus billion people on earth went to church on Sabbath?
   The Sabbath commemorates God as the Creator of heaven and earth. If all 7 plus billion people on earth went to church on Sabbath, the following belief systems would not exist: atheism, agnosticism, evolution, Buddhism, Hinduism, etc. Because all would be worshipping the true God.

6. Was the Sabbath made just for the Jews? Mark 2:27
   No, it was made for man. M-A-N is a strange way to spell Jews. Besides, Adam and Eve were not Jews. Abraham was the first Jew and that was in Genesis 12, about 2,500 years after Adam and Eve's time. **See Supplement 10-B**

7. Did Jesus keep the Sabbath? Luke 4:14-16; 1 Peter 2:21
   Luke 4:14-16 – Yes, Jesus did. He had a habit (or custom) of going to church on Sabbath.
   1 Peter 2:21 – Since Jesus is our Example, we should do what He did.

8. Did Jesus' disciples keep the Sabbath after Jesus died? Luke 23:54-56; Acts 13:42-44; 18:4,11
   Yes, they did.

9. On which day did Jesus rise from the grave? Matthew 28:1-6; Mark 16:1-6,9; Luke 24:1-6; John 20:1-7
   On the first day of the week.

10. Will the Sabbath be kept in heaven? Isaiah 66:22,23
    Yes, it will be kept in heaven. So, the Sabbath was kept from Creation Week, throughout the Old Testament, throughout the New Testament by Jesus and His disciples and by Gentiles (non-Jews), and the Sabbath will be kept in heaven. Yet, many Christians believe we are to keep Sunday today. To be consistent, we will keep the Sabbath. Keeping Sunday is not consistent with the Bible.

Do you understand that the Bible Sabbath is Saturday, the seventh day of the week?

Days of the Week
Lesson 10-A

The information below was taken from *The World Book Encyclopedia*, 1986 edition:

SUNDAY   Sunday is the first day of the week among Christian peoples. It is the day set aside for rest and worship of God. Sunday was the day sacred to the sun among Teutonic peoples, and its name mean the "day of the sun."

MONDAY   Monday is the second day of the week. The word comes from the Anglo-Saxon monandaeg, which means moon's day.

TUESDAY   Tuesday is the name of the third day of the week. Its name comes from Tiu, or Tiw, the old Anglo-Saxon form of Tyr, name of the Norse god of war. Tyr was the son of Odin, or Woden, for whom Wednesday was named.

WEDNESDAY   Wednesday is the English name for the fourth day of the week. This day gets its name from Woden, or Odin, the chief god in Teutonic mythology, to whom it was sacred...The first to name the days of the week after gods in mythology were the ancient Romans. They called the fourth day of the week after the god of Mercury.

THURSDAY   Thursday is the fifth day of the week. The ancient Norsemen considered the day sacred to Thor, the Teutonic god of thunder. The name mean's Thor's day.

FRIDAY   Friday is the sixth day of the week. The name comes from the Anglo-Saxon word Frigedaeg, which means Frigg's day. Frigg was goddess of love in Norse mythology.

SATURDAY   Saturday, called Saeter-daeg by the Anglo-Saxons, is the seventh day of the week. It is named for the Roman god of Saturn.

Has the Week Cycle Been Broken?
Lesson 10-B

I. **Has the weekly cycle of seven days remained unbroken since the beginning of the world?**

   a. Genesis 1, 2- These two chapters establish the Creation Week with the Sabbath occurring every seven days. Bible scholars and creationists believe the world was created by God around 4004 B.C.

   b. Exodus 16:4-30- Here we find God re-establishing the seven-day cycle with His people. During their long captivity in Egypt they lost track of time (Exodus 12:40, 41). It was God's purpose that they knew about His Sabbath. The Israelites did not think of God's Sabbath because they got accustomed to the Egyptian lifestyle. Jacob took 70 souls into Egypt 430 years before. Moses' generation knew nothing about the Sabbath. So, God re-established His Sabbath with His people. This took place in 1490 B.C.

   c. Exodus 20:8-11 – When God gave the Ten Commandment Law at Mount Sinai, He required the people to observe the weekly Sabbath. When consistently observed, it keeps intact the weekly cycle of seven days.

   d. The following passages present evidence that the weekly cycle continued without interruption throughout the Old and New Testaments (all of the verses mention the Sabbath but notice God did not have to remind them that it's the seventh day; the years are given to show the consistency of Sabbath keeping):

      1. 1 Chronicles 9:32 – 1200 BC
      2. 2 Kings 11:6, 7, 9 – 885 BC
      3. Isaiah 58:13, 14 – 700 BC
      4. Ezekiel 20:12, 20 – 590 BC
      5. Mark 2:27, 28 – AD 29 (AD stands for Anno Domini which is Latin for "in the year of our Lord"; it does not mean "*after death.*"
      6. Luke 4:14-16 – AD 27
      7. Luke 23:53-24:1 – AD 31
      8. Acts 13:42-44; 18:4 – AD 55
      9. Revelation 1:10 – AD 95

We have seen from the above points that the weekly cycle has remained intact from Creation until the end of the New Testament. That means the seven-day cycle has been unbroken for over four thousand years (4004 BC – AD 95). Has the weekly cycle lost its sequence during the last two thousand years (from Jesus' time to now)? This brings us down to our day.

I. **Let's see what astronomers have to say:**

1. "One essential point is that of the continuity of the week. The majority of the members of the Office of Longitudes considered that the reform of the calendar should not be based on the breaking of this continuity. They considered that it would be highly undesirable to interrupt a continuity which has existed for so many centuries." —M. Emile Picard, president of the Office of Longitudes, *Report on the Reform of the Calendar*, p. 51, August 17, 1926.

2. "The regular sequence of weeks, which have now been running without a break for some three thousand years has proceeded in absolutely invariable manner since what may be called the dawn of history."—- *Our Astronomical Column*, June 6, 1931.

II. **What do the Orthodox Jews say about the seventh day being the Sabbath:**

1. On any Saturday morning take a ride around town to see who is going to church on that day. You are going to run into some Orthodox Jews who have an accurate record of time at least since the time of Christ. Why do I say 'accurate?' His father kept the Sabbath and his father kept the Sabbath all the way back to Christ's day a least. Orthodox Jews are the strict ones. They have a true account of which day is the Seventh Day of the week.

The Only Calendar Change
Lesson 10-C

JULIAN 1582	October				Gregorian 1582	
Sun	Mon	Tues	Wed	Thurs	Fri	Sat
	1	2	3	4	15	16
17	18	19	20	21	22	23
24	25	26	27	28	29	30
31						

The Gregorian Calendar, also known as the Western or Christian Calendar, is the most widely used calendar in the world today. Its predecessor, the Julian Calendar, was replaced because it did not properly reflect the actual time it takes the Earth to circle once around the Sun, known as a tropical year.

Since the Gregorian **calendar** accounted more accurately for leap years, it was **11 days** ahead of the Julian **calendar** by **1752**. To correct this discrepancy and align all dates, **11 days had** to be dropped when the switch was made. Those 11 days were dropped during the month of September.

The Change of the Sabbath
Lesson 11

1. Did God the Father change the Sabbath? Exodus 20:8-11; 31:18; Psalm 89:34; Deuteronomy 4:2
   Exodus 20:8-11 – No.
   Exodus 31:18 – No, God wrote on tables of stone, writing on stone is permanent.
   Psalm 89:34 – God will not alter what He speaks. He spoke the Ten Commandments (Exodus 20:1-17).

2. Did Jesus change the Sabbath? Luke 4:14-16; Matthew 5:17,18
   Luke 4:14-16 – Jesus had a habit of keeping the Sabbath.
   Matthew 5:17, 18 – Jesus did not change the Law.

3. Did the disciples change God's Sabbath? Acts 13:42-44; 16:13; 18:4,11; Revelation 1:10
   Acts 13:42-44 – No.
   Acts 16:13 – No.
   Acts 18:4, 11 – No.
   Revelation 1:10 – No.

4. How does God feel about those who disrespect His Sabbath? Ezekiel 22:26,28
   God is displeased when the priests disrespect His Sabbath. Because the priests stand in God's place, when they are profane (unholy) they make God look unholy. And in verse 28, the disobedient priests preach lies and then say, "Thus saith God, when the Lord hath not spoken."

5. Is breaking just one of God's commandments really all that bad? James 2:8-12
   Yes, the Ten Commandments are like links in a bicycle chain. If one link breaks, bike riding is over. If I break one of the Ten Commandments, it's over for me.

6. If God the Father, Jesus, nor His disciples changed the Sabbath, who did? Daniel 7:25
   Man. Question 7 gives more detail to this question.

7. What are some of the characteristics of the power spoken of in Daniel 7:25? vs. 8,24,25
   See Supplement 11-A-C

8. How will God deal with my deceased relatives and friends who faithfully went to church on Sunday? Acts 17:30
   They will be saved if they didn't know about the Sabbath.

9. What does Jesus say to me if I hold unto family tradition? Matthew 15:3,9,13; John 3:19,20
   Matthew 15:3,9,13 – We should not follow tradition if it goes against God's Word. And if God didn't plant it (He didn't plant Sunday), it will be uprooted.
   John 3:19,20 – We should follow the light not darkness.

10. To whom should I give all of my allegiance? Acts 5:29
    God and God alone.

Do you understand that the Sabbath was changed by MAN and not by GOD?

Is it your desire to consider keeping God's seventh day Sabbath?

Teacher's Guide

The Beasts of Daniel 7
Lesson 11-A

THE FOUR BEASTS

1. Lion (vs. 4) – BABYLON- 606 BC- 538 BC
2. Bear (vs. 5) – MEDO-PERSIA- 538 BC- 331 BC
3. Leopard (vs. 6) – GRECIA- 331 BC- 168 BC
4. Dreadful Beast (vs. 7) – ROME- 168 BC- AD 476

THE TEN HORNS OF DANIEL 7:7

1. Alamanni (Germany)
2. Anglo-Saxons (England)
3. Burgundians (Switzerland)
4. Franks (France)
5. Lombards (Italy)
6. Suevi (Portugal)
7. Visigoths (Spain)
8. Heruli (Destroyed)
9. Ostrogoths (Destroyed)
10. Vandals (Destroyed)

EIGHT CHARACTERISTS OF THE "LITTLE HORN" IN DANIEL 7:8

1. "came up among the ten" – vs. 8
2. "he shall rise after the ten" – vs. 24
3. "three of the first horns plucked up" – vs. 84.
4. "he shall be diverse from the first [horn]" – vs. 24
5. "he shall speak great words against the Most High" – vs. 25 ["blasphemies"- Revelation 13:5]. What is a form of blasphemy? A. Luke 5:20,21; B. John 10:30-33
6. "he shall wear out [persecute] the saints" – vs. 25
7. "he shall think to change times and laws" – vs. 25
8. "given into his hand until a time and time and the dividing of time" [to rule for 1260 years] – vs. 25

Factors that Led to Sunday Worship
Lesson 11-B

THE PASCAL/EASTER CONTROVERSY

a. During the time of Pope Sixtus (AD 125), Gentile Christians celebrated the resurrection of Christ on Sunday; around the same time the Jewish Christians commemorated the Passover (always on the 14th of Nisan-the first month of the Jewish year). Both went to church on Sabbath until the following took place:
"On the day called Sunday there is an assemblage of all who live in the cities or the country, and the memoirs of the apostles, or the writings of the prophets are read so long as there is time…And we all in common make our assembly on Sunday, since it is the first day in which God changed the darkness and matter and made the world and Jesus Christ our Saviour rose from the dead on the same day."—Justin Martyr, *First Apology*, chapter 67, AD 155.

THE JEWISH REVOLT

a. "In AD 132 a new revolt broke out and the independence of Judea was proclaimed under a messianic claimant who is commonly known as Bar Cocheba. After three years of guerilla fighting [with the Romans] this rising was crushed."—F.F. Bruce, *Second Thoughts on the Dead Sea Scrolls*, pp. 11-13, 1956. As a result of this revolt Jews and Judaism were discredited. To avoid possible Roman retaliation, Gentile Christians separated themselves from the Jews during this time.

THE SABBATH FAST

a. "That the Sabbath is for fasting the clearest argument demonstrates. For if we not only celebrate the Lord's Day [Sunday] on account of the resurrection of our Lord Jesus Christ as Easter, but also throughout each recurring cycle of the weeks, we repeat the image of this very day, and fast on Sabbath."—Pope Innocent I (AD 402-417), *Epistle 25*, chapter 4.

b. In referring to this same era, the following is recorded:
"In the Western Churches, particularly the Roman [Catholic churches], where opposition produced the custom of celebrating Saturday in particular as a fast day."—Augustus Neander, *The History of the Christian Religion and Church*, p. 186, 1943

CONSTANTINE'S FAMOUS SUNDAY EDICT ON MARCH 7, 321 AD
"On the venerable Day of the Sun, let all magistrates and people residing in cities rest, and let all workshops be closed. In the country, however, persons engaged in agriculture may freely and lawfully continue their pursuits; because it often happens

that another day is not so suitable for grain-sowing or for vine-planting; lest by neglecting the proper moment for such operations the bounty of heaven should be lost."—History of the Christian Church, Volume 3 (5th Edition; New York: Scribner, 1902), p. 380.

A Power that Opposes and Exalts Himself above God
Lesson 11-C

"Who opposeth and exalteth himself above all that is called God, or that is worshipped; so that he as God sitteth in the temple of God, shewing himself that he is God."—2 Thessalonians 2:4

WHAT EARTHLY POWER DARED TO DO THIS?
"All names which in the Scriptures are applied to Christ, by virtue of which it is established that He is over the church, all the same names are applied to the Pope." —Robert Bellarmine, *Disputations de Controversilis*, chapter 17.

"For not man, but God separates those whom the Roman Pontiff (who exercises the functions, not of mere man, but of the true God), having weighed the necessity or benefit of the churches, dissolves, not by human but rather by divine authority." —The Decretals of Gregory IX, Book 1, chapter 3, *Corpus Juris Canonici*.

"The pope is the supreme judge of the law of the land...He is the vicegerent of Christ, who is not only a Priest forever, but also King of Kings and Lord of Lords." —*La Civilta Cattolica*, March 18, 1871.

"They have assumed infallibility, which belongs only to God. They profess to forgive sins, which belongs only to God. They profess to open and shut heaven, which belongs only to God. They profess to be higher than all the kings of earth, which belongs only to God. And they go beyond God in pretending to loose whole nations from their oath of allegiance to their kings, when such kings do not please them. And they go against God, when they give indulgences for sin."
—Adam Clark, *Commentary*, on Daniel 7:25.

Prayer
Lesson 12

1. What is prayer?
   Talking with God. As our prayer lives get stronger, we should talk to God as we would a trusting friend. When a gentleman and a lady first go on a date they don't tell each other all about themselves (at least they should not) that comes in time. It is the same way with God. As our relationship with God mature so will the nature of our conversation or prayers with Him mature.

2. Why is prayer necessary for me? Luke 22:46; 1 Peter 4:7
   Luke 22:46 – Prayers helps us to resist temptation.
   1 Peter 4:7 – Pray more now because we are living in the last days.

3. What should be my position in prayer? Psalm 95:6
   I should kneel during my personal prayers.

4. What is one important condition as I begin to pray? Matthew 21:21,22
   We should have faith. What good is it if we pray and don't believe God is going to do what is best for us? We must have faith.

5. Why is it necessary for me to pray in Jesus' name? John 16:23; John 14:6
   John 16:23 – Because Jesus died for us, we should pray in His name when talking to God the Father.
   John 14:6 – Without Jesus, we cannot approach God.

6. What should be my attitude in prayer? 2 Chronicles 7:14
   We should be humble. God is God, He is not a man (see Isaiah 55:8,9).

7. Where is the best place for me to pray? Matthew 6:6; Mark 1:35
   In private. Family prayer and prayer with my spouse is very important but to really grow as a Christian we need personal time with God.

8. Why must I be persistent in prayer? Luke 11:5-9
God sees how serious I am about getting what I ask (or whatever He thinks is best) and He will answer according to His will.

9. What happens if I pray to God with a proud heart? Luke 18:9-14
Nothing, God will not answer. I should always be humble.

10. How should I handle my enimies in prayer? Matthew 5:44; 6:14,15
Matthew 5:44 – If we can pray for those who, despitefully, use us, our Christian walk will be taken to another level.
Matthew 6:14,15 – If we want God to forgive us when we sin, we must forgive others. If we don't forgive others neither will God forgive us of our sins.

11. How often should I pray? Psalm 55:17; 1 Thessalonians 5:17
Psalm 55:17 – Three times a day.
1 Thessalonians 5:17 – Pray without ceasing.
There is no contradiction between praying three times a day and praying without ceasing. We should pray two to three times day in private kneeling but I should have an attitude of prayer all day and talk to God in the car, at work, at school, etc. and that's praying without ceasing.

12. What is the result of faithful prayer? James 5:16
God will answer!

Do you believe that prayer is vital for the Christian?

If you don't already, are you willing to make prayer a daily practice?

Sabbath Observance
Lesson 13

1. What did God say about the seventh day Sabbath in the commandments? Exodus 20:8
   To keep it holy.

2. When does the Sabbath begin? Genesis 1:31-2:2; Mark 1:32
   At sunset on the 6th day of the week (Friday).
   Bible Instructor: Many like to use the last part of Leviticus 23:32. You can use it if you chose but be prepared to explain the rest of the verse if the student asks. And the rest of the verse has nothing to do with when the sun sets on Sabbath.

3. What did God tell Moses to build and for what purpose? Exodus 25:8
   God told Moses to build a sanctuary so that He could be closer to His people.

4. Why should I go to church on Sabbath rather than stay at home? Psalm 92:12, 13; Psalm 122:1; Hebrews 10:25
   We grow spiritually in the sanctuary. We praise God there and we fellowship with the saints.

5. What did Jesus do on God's holy day? Luke 4:14-16; 1 Peter 2:21
   Luke 4:14-16 – Jesus went to church (as seen in lesson 10)
   1 Peter 2:21 – Jesus was our example and if He went to church on the seventh day Sabbath, what should we do? Go to church on the seventh day Sabbath.

6. How should I conduct myself on the Sabbath? Isaiah 58:13,14
   We should not do nor attend non-spiritual events. Events such as sports, school, theatre, and business transactions are forbidden.

7. Is it okay for me to go to the malls and grocery stores on the Sabbath after I get out of church? Nehemiah 10:31
   We should not buy and sell on the Sabbath.

8. Can I go to my job and work on the Sabbath? Exodus 20:8-11; Ezechiel 46:2
   Exodus 20:8-11 – I should not work on God's Sabbath.
   Ezekiel 46:1 – Sunday is a working day.

9. Should doctors and nurses work on the Sabbath? Matthew 12:9-14
   It's good to do well on the Sabbath. Some medical, and police folks work on the Sabbath and some do not.

10. What did Jesus mean by "the Sabbath was made for man and not man for the Sabbath?" Mark 2:27,28
    The Sabbath was made to be a blessing for man; man was not created to be a blessing for the Sabbath. God pours out showers of blessings on the Sabbath that can strengthen us as Christians and when we disobey the Sabbath by doing our thing, we don't receive those blessings.

Do you understand how we are to honor God on His holy day?

If you don't already, would you be willing to keep holy the upcoming Sabbath?

The Gift of Prophecy
Lesson 14

1. What are some of the gifts of the Holy Spirit? 1 Corinthians 12:28
    Prophets, teachers, healing, etc. (the gift of 'governments' are leaders)

2. What is the purpose of these gifts? 1 Corinthians 12:7; Ephesians 4:11,12
    To build up the church

3. Will all the gifts remain in the church until Jesus comes? 1 Corinthians 1:7
    Yes, including prophets (the student can see that the gifts, including prophets, will be needed in the last days to keep the church strong. All the gifts extend beyond when John completed writing the book of Revelation)

4. What are two of the identifying marks of the remnant church? Revelation 12:17
    Remnant – the last part or the remaining portion of the original; the remnant church is the last part of the original church that began with Jesus and the 12 disciples. Like at a fabric store; a remnant sale is the sale of the last part of the original yarn (same color, same texture of the original but the remaining portion).
    1. They keep all ten of God's Commandments
    2. They have the testimony of Jesus

    a. What is the "testimony of Jesus and who had it? Revelation 19:10
    The testimony of Jesus is the spirit of prophecy. Those who had were the brethren or the fellow-servants

    b. Who is the "fellow-servant" or the "brethren?" Revelation 22:8,9
    The fellow-servant or the brethren were the prophets, verse 9. Combining all parts of this question, the testimony of Jesus has something to do with the gift of prophecy being present in the church. No wonder the devil is so angry with the church, they keep all Ten Commandments and they have a prophet to point out his deceptions.

5. How important are prophets? Amos 3:7; 2 Chronicles 20:20
    Prophets are very important. We would know nothing of God's goodness, greatness, and love if it were not for prophets because there would be no Bible. Maybe we might know something intuitive (how you feel), maybe.

6. Does the Bible pin-point the gift of prophecy in the last days? Acts 2:17,18
   Yes (another verse showing that God will have prophets in the last days, after the Bible was completed. Too many Christians believe that there are no prophets after John wrote the book of Revelation).

7. Must a prophet write a book in the Bible for him/her to be authoritative and true? I Kings 18:36-40; Acts 21:10,11,27-30
   No (the student needs to see that to be a true prophet of God, you do not have to write a book in the Bible)

8. Did prophets write other books that are not in the Bible? 2 Chronicles 9:29; Colossians 4:16
   Yes (the student needs to see that prophets wrote other books that were not included in the Bible and yet they can still be true prophets; you're paving the way for other true prophets (such as Ellen White) who may write books that are not in the Bible but whose books are in harmony with the Bible).

9. What are the four tests of a TRUE PROPHET?

   1) 1 John 4:1,2; Colossians 2:6,9 – believe that Jesus came in the flesh and that He is divine

   2) Isaiah 8:20 – what the prophet says and write must be in harmony with the Bible

   3) Jeremiah 28:9 – the prophecies or predictions the prophets make must "come to pass" or happen because if they are of God, He knows the future

   4) Matthew 7:15-20 – the prophet must live an exemplary life; yes, they all make mistakes but they must be an example.

   See Supplement 14-A

Teacher's Guide

The Gift of Prophecy
Lesson 14-A

The Seventh-day Adventist Church believes that Ellen G. White was given the gift of prophecy from God. Therefore, we believe she was a prophet of God. Born on November 26, 1827, at Gorham, Maine, Ellen Gould Harmon followed an uneventful life until she was nine years old. At that age she was hit in the face with a rock thrown by a classmate. As a result of the accident, she could hardly breathe through her nose. Afflicted with a bad cough, Ellen was forced to discontinue her education after receiving only three years of formal schooling.

At the age of 17, she received her first vision (December, 1844). Ellen White, like anyone else who is called a prophet, must pass the four biblical tests of a TRUE prophet before she can be called one.

TEST 1   **1 John 4:2** – "Every spirit that confesseth that Jesus Christ is come in the flesh is of God."

What did Ellen White believe about Jesus?

"Christ was treated as we deserve, that we might be treated as He deserves. He was condemned for our sins, in which He had no share, that we might be justified by His righteousness, in which we had no share. He suffered the death, which was ours, that we might receive the life, which was His. 'With His stripes we are healed.'" —*Desire of Ages*, p. 25

"We, Adventists, are believers in Christ, in His divinity and in His pre-existence. —*Testimonies to the Church*, vol. 6, p. 58

TEST 2   **Isaiah 8:20** – "To the law and to the testimony: if they speak not according to this word, it is because there in no light in them."

What did Ellen White believe about the Bible?

"The Holy Scriptures are to be accepted as an authoritative, infallible revelation of His will. They are the standard of character, the revealer of doctrines, and the test of experience." —Introduction to the *Great Controversy*, p. vii.

"The central theme of the Bible, the theme about which every other in the book clusters, is the redemption plan, the restoration in the human soul of the image of God. The burden of every book and every passage of the Bible is the unfolding of this wondrous theme—man's uplifting." —*Education*, pp. 125,126.

TEST 3   **Jeremiah 28:9** – "When the word of the prophet shall come to pass, then shall the prophet be known, that the Lord hath truly sent him."

Did Ellen White's predictions come true? In the left column you'll notice Ellen White's prophecy and in the right column you'll see its fulfillment the last one is not in columns (only four are given).

DISASTER

E. G. White—1902
"Not long hence these cities will suffer under the judgment of God. San Francisco and Oakland are becoming as Sodom and Gomorrah, and the Lord will visit them in wrath."
—*Evangelism*, pp. 403,404.

Andrew C. Lawson—1906
"On April 18, 1906, shortly after 5:00 a.m., a great earthquake struck San Francisco and long narrow band of towns, villages, and countryside to the north-northwest and south-southeast. Many buildings were wrecked; hundreds of people were killed." —*The California Earthquake of April 18, 1906*. Report of the State Earthquake Investigation Commission, Carnegie Institution of Washington, 1908, vol. 1 pp. 451.

TOBACCO AND DISEASE

E. G. White—1864
"Tobacco is a poison of the most deceitful and malignant kind, having an exciting, then a paralyzing influence upon the body. It is all the more dangerous because its effects upon the system are so slow, and at first scarcely perceivable. Multitudes have fallen victims to its poisonous influence. They have surely murdered themselves by this slow poison." —*Temperance*, p. 57

Alton Oshsner, M.D.—1957
"In 1957 the American Cancer Society (along with three other organizations), appointed a committee of seven scientists to study and evaluate all the available data regarding the effects smoking on health. These scientists were chosen because of their integrity and ability to analyze critically experimental and clinical investigations. After an intense study of one year, they concluded: "'The sum total of scientific evidence establishes beyond reasonable doubt that cigarette smoking is a causative factor in the rapidly increasing incidence of human epidermoid carcinoma of the lung.'" —*Smoking on Health*, pp. 40,41.

PRENATAL INFLUENCE

E. G. White—1865

"The irritability, nervousness and despondency, manifested by the mother, will mark the character of her child. In past generations, if mothers had informed themselves in regard to the laws of their being, they would have understood that their constitutional strength, as well as their morals, and their mental faculties, would in a great measure be represented in their offspring." —*Selected Messages*, Book 2, p. 431

Ashley Montagu, M.D.—1954

"For years scientists have believed that your unborn baby lives an insulated existence, protected from all external influence, but this in not true. It is exciting news that you can control the development of your unborn child. Nothing is more important than the health and well-being of the mother. —*Ladies Home Journal*, February, 1954, p. 43

THE COLLAPSE OF THE WORLD TRADE CENTER ON SEPTEMBER 11, 2001

Ellen G. White—1909

"On one occasion, when in New York City, I was in the night season called upon to behold buildings rising story after story toward heaven. These buildings were warranted to be fireproof, and they were erected to glorify the owners and builders. Higher and still higher these buildings rose, and in them the most costly material was used. Those to whom these buildings belonged were not asking themselves: 'How can we best glorify God?' The Lord was not in their thoughts.

"I thought: 'Oh, that those who are thus investing their means could see their course as God sees it! They are piling up magnificent buildings, but how foolish in the sight of the Ruler of the universe is their planning and devising. They are not studying with all the powers of heart and mind how they may glorify God. They have lost sight of this, the first duty of man.'

"As these lofty buildings went up, the owners rejoiced with ambitious pride that they had money to use in gratifying self and provoking the envy of their neighbors. Much of the money that they thus invested had been obtained through exaction, through grinding down the poor. They forgot that in heaven an account of every business transaction is kept; every unjust deal, every fraudulent act, is there recorded. The time is coming when in their fraud and insolence men will reach a point that the Lord will not permit them to pass, and they will learn that there is a limit to the forbearance of Jehovah.

"The scene that next passed before me was an alarm of fire. Men looked at the lofty and supposedly fire-proof buildings and said: 'They are perfectly safe.' But these buildings were consumed as if made of pitch. **The fire engines could do nothing to stay the destruction. The firemen were unable to operate the engines.**" —*Testimonies to the Church*, Volume 9, p. 12,13.

James Nachtwey—2001
"The creation of our photography agency VII had just been announced and on September 10

[2001], I left Paris for New York. I arrived home about 11 o'clock that night and the next morning, as I was making coffee, I heard what sounded like a piece of steel hitting my roof. I looked out of my window, where I had a clear view of the World Trade Center, and saw black smoke billowing out of the south tower. As I was organizing my cameras and film, I heard another loud sound. I looked out of my window again and saw that now the north tower was burning as well.

"I made my way through the crowd of fleeing people and began to photograph the wounded being helped along by firemen and paramedics or lying by the side of the street waiting for assistance. I was not yet aware that the towers had been hit by airplanes, but it seemed clear that this was a terrorist attack. As I was framing the south tower with the cross of a nearby church in the foreground, the skyscraper collapsed. The massive cloud of smoke and ash was filled with glass and steel as it raced through the canyons of lower Manhattan.

"What had just happened seemed unbelievable to me, and I knew I had to photograph the wreckage of the tower lying on the ground. I made my way through the smoke and approached what looked like the set of a science fiction movie about the Apocalypse [end of the world]. Except for two other photographers, the scene was deserted and the skeleton of one of the mightiest skyscrapers on earth lay twisted and broken on the street. **Fire trucks and police cars were crushed and burning, their emergency flashers still blinking on and off.**" —At the Heart of Ground Zero, *Sunday Herald,* September 2002.

TEST 4   Matthew 7:15-20 – "Wherefore by their fruits ye shall know them."

What was Ellen White like? Did she have a burden to win souls for Christ? Did she lead any people to Christ?

Here is what one writer said about Mrs. White, just twelve months before her death:
"This remarkable woman, also, though almost entirely self-educated, has written and published more books and in more languages, which circulate to a greater extent than the written works of any woman in history." —George Wharton Jones, *California—Romantic and Beautiful,* p. 320.

The editor of a leading religious journal made this comment after her death:
"Here is a noble record, and she deserves great honor. She show no spirited pride and she sought no 'filthy lucre' (riches). She did the work of a worthy prophetess." —*The New York Independent,* August 23, 1915.

Thomas M. Elliot, a former editor of the prestigious Atlantic Constitution, wrote an editorial in his paper on October 9, 1950, endorsing two books written by Ellen G. White:
"Among the hundreds of books, I have studied on the subject of religion that inspire heart warmth and enriched faith, none have been of greater help than Ellen G. White's two books—*Patriarchs and Prophets* and *Prophets and Kings.* These books were written, not for literary fame or financial reward, but to help heart-hungry humanity learn of God. They make God's dealings

with men clear to the most simple-minded reader without bias. I commend these books to all seekers after a clearer knowledge of the righteousness of God."

A testimony for the book Education was given by Dr. Florence Stratemeyer, a noted educator: "Recently the book *Education* by Ellen G. White has been brought to my attention. Written at the turn of the century, this volume was more than fifty years ahead of its time. And I was surprised to learn that it was written by a woman with but three years of schooling. The breadth and depth of its philosophy amazed me. Its concept of balanced education, harmonious development, and thinking and acting on principle are advanced educational concepts. The objective of restoring in man the image of God, the teaching of parental responsibility, and emphasis on self-control in the child are ideals the world desperately needs." —Florence Stratemeyer, Professor of Education, Teachers College, Columbia University, New York City, 1959.

Do you believe Ellen White had the gift of prophecy?

Substitution
Lesson 15

1. What is a substitute?
    Any answer along the line of a person who stands in place of another.

2. Describe how a lamb or a bullock was used as the sinner's substitute? Leviticus 4:28-30
    The sinner brings the sacrifice to the sanctuary. The priest examines it make sure it has no cuts, bruises, etc. (after all is does represent Jesus). The sinner lays his hands on the sacrifice and confess' its sins and as he does this a transference takes place; the sinner transfers his guilt to the innocent sacrifice and the sacrifice transfers its innocence to the guilty sinner. The priest gives the sinner the knife and the sinner kills the sacrifice that is guilty of his sin.

3. Why would I need a substitute? Genesis 3:1-7; Romans 3:23; 6:23
    Because man had fallen into sin.

4. Who is worthy to be my substitute and what makes this person worthy? Matthew 1:21; Romans 5:8; Revelation 13:8
    Jesus, because He died for us.

5. Why didn't man die for mankind and become his substitute?
    1 Corinthians 6:19, 20
    The life man has is not his own. God gave man life so man can't take it and give to another person.

6. Why didn't angels die for guilty man and become his substitute? Psalm 103:20; Matthew 4:9,10
    Psalm 103:20 – Angels are obedient to the Ten Commandments therefore they cannot die for the breaking of the Ten Commandments.
    Matthew 4:9,10 – If angels had died for man, they would be worthy of man's worship. And God could not tolerate angels receiving worship.

7. Why did Jesus do it? Why did He decide to be my substitute? Jeremiah 31:3; John 3:16; 15:13
    Jesus was moved by His love for us; no one made Him do it.

8. How can I make Jesus my personal substitute? Revelation 3:20; 2 Corinthians 5:15, 17
    By inviting Him into my heart.

9. What is the role of God the Father in my salvation? 1 Timothy 2:4; 2 Peter 3:9; 2 Corinthians 5:19
    God wants all people to be saved. God was in Christ reconciling (rejoining) us to Himself.

10. What is the role of God the Holy Spirit in my salvation? John 16:7-11; Acts 1:8
    The Holy Spirit convicts us of sin and He empower us to live like a Christian and He empowers us to share Jesus with people.

Do you understand that Jesus is your Substitute?

God's Dress Code
Lesson 16

1. In addition to setting up the seventh day Sabbath before the Fall, what other institution did God establish? Did God use the "wedding band" to seal the holy marriage? Genesis 2:21-25

    First question – Marriage. Second question– No, Eve had natural beauty; she did not need anything artificial to help her looks; no jewelry.
    Note: The wedding band did not start with God or in the church. **The wedding ring came from outside the church.**

2. After man sinned, what was his first piece of clothing? Genesis 3:7
    Fig leaves. No jewelry.

3. What did Jacob tell his household to do with their earrings and strange (idol) gods? Genesis 35:1-4

    The background to this passage is Genesis 28, where Jacob was running from his brother Esau. Jacob came to a place where he fell asleep and he had a dream of angels ascending and descending upon a ladder. This place Jacob named Bethel. Bethel means "house of God" or "place of God." God told Jacob if you are going into a place you name in My honor, you have to get rid of some things. Idols and jewelry were those things. Jacob buried them near Shechem. The idols and jewelry came from Rachel's servants. Rachel had servants because her father, Laban, was wealthy and an idol worshipper.
    Note: The jewelry that the servants had did not come from God's people; it came from people who did not worship God. **Jewelry came from outside the church.**

4. What was one reason that God called the children of Israel "stiffnecked" (stubborn)? Exodus 32:1-4; 33:1-6

    God called them stiffnecked because they took their jewelry and melted it down to make a golden calf, an idol god to worship. After God talked to them, the people took off their ornaments.
    Note: The jewelry and ornaments came from their 430 year stay in Egypt. They were influenced by the Egyptian lifestyle and had lost sight of what God expects of His people. The mixed multitude, Egyptians who left Egypt with Israel, were a negative influence on the Israelites as well (Exodus 12:38). **Ornaments came from outside the church.**

5. What did the Israelites do with the jewelry they had obtained from being victorious in battle? Numbers 31:48-51
   They sacrificed the jewelry. They did not put it on.

6. Who did Ahab, the king of Judah, marry? 1 Kings 16:29-31. How is she described and what happened to her? 2 Kings 9:30-36
   First question – Jezebel. King Ahab married outside of the church and unconverted Jezebel brought her lifestyle with her. Second question – She painted her face, something similar to makeup and her body parts were eaten by dogs. **Make-up came from outside the church.**

7. Why did God curse the "daughters of Zion?" Isaiah 3:16-24; Ezekiel 5:5
   Isaiah 3:16-24 – God cursed the daughters of Zion because they were negatively influenced by the heathen nations around them and adorned themselves with their ornaments and jewels.
   Ezekiel 5:5 – God had placed His people in the middle of the heathen nations so they could be a light and lead them to the true God. But instead of that happening, God's people were influence by the heathen and took on their practices.

8. What does the Bible say about tattoos? Leviticus 19:28
   God's people should not get piercing or tattoos on their body.

9. What does the New Testament say about the wearing of jewelry? 1 Timothy 2:9,10; 1 Peter 3:3,4 Women should dress modestly and not wear jewelry and other ornaments. **See Supplement 16-A.** In the New Testament in Greece and Rome, wealthy women braided their hair and they weaved strands of gold and silver in it for personal attention and to look down on those who couldn't afford to do it. A violation of verse 2 where Peter says the wife or woman should be chaste. This means pure in conduct and in style.

10. How does the book of Revelation picture the woman who represents God's true church? Revelation 12:1
    She was virtuous and like Eve, adorned with natural beauty, the sun and the moon.

11. How does Jesus compare Solomon and all of his glory to the lilies of the field? Matthew 6:25-29
    Of all the lilies of the field, Solomon in all glory (gold, silver, etc.), was not arrayed like one lily. God values the natural above the artificial. If God says that about a lily, what about us who are made in His image?

12. How did the Israelites respond when Gideon asked them to surrender the earrings of

the Ishmaelites? Judges 8:24,25
The willingly gave them up.

Do you understand that God has a standard on how we should dress?

Standards of Apparel
Lesson 16-A

Creation is not only complex but it is also beautiful. Innumerable forms, colors, and sounds are manifested in flowers, birds, animals, plants, mountains, trees, and most completely in human beings point to the greatest artist of all—God. Human life is destined for beauty and happiness, and hence, the natural heart is bent to admire and seek beauty (Genesis 2:9). The virtue and righteousness is gone from the race. Little do men and women reflect the grace of the Creator. Crooked and distorted, dwarfed and ill-proportioned, and burnt and bleached, man's body reflects his evil estate. The man and the woman whom we think most beautiful would look like monsters in the presence of Adam and Eve in their perfect condition. Their innocence gone the holy pair, shivering and cringing in the nakedness of sin, sewed fig leaves together to cover themselves. And as the peace and purity of the race declined, men and women more and more sought to hide their loss with inventions of fabrics and fashions with glittering gold and jewels of the mine. The further from grace they fell the more they decorated themselves, replacing the beautiful simplicity of their innocence with the flashy colors of their inventions (Ecclesiastes 7:29). That which was the symbol of man's shame (sheep skins) he made the medium of his pride. The less elevated his thoughts and the less pure his purpose, the heavier his wardrobe and the richer his jewels.

GENERAL PRINCIPLES

I. **Principle of Modesty – 1 Timothy 2:9**
Christians will not shock or dazzle onlookers, nor will they dress to attract attention. Extremes that display one's body or affluence contradict the Christian sense of decorum and decency.

II. **Principle of Inward Beauty – 1 Peter 3:3,4**
This turns our admiration from colors and styles to the heart. Outward beauty is only skin deep and its attraction only temporary. The inward beauty of character—the beauty of harmonious, peaceful, and benevolent disposition—is lasting and is real beauty.

III. **Self-Esteem – Genesis 1:26,27**
Our self-esteem should be rooted in the fact that God created us in His image. In addition to stroking our self-esteem by saying we were made a little lower than the angels, God crowned us with honor and glory (Psalm 8:4,5).

Must Christians Speak in Tongues?
Lesson 17

1. What is the origin of different tongues? Genesis 11:1-9 A tongue is a language like; English, Spanish, and French.
   At the tower of Babel. Before this, the earth had just one language. The different languages that occurred at the tower of Babel were languages people understood.

2. List some of the gifts of the Holy Spirit? 1 Corinthians 12:28
   Pastor, prophet, teacher, gift of tongues, etc.

3. Do all have the gift of tongues? 1 Corinthians 12:28-30
   No. This is important because those who believe in speaking in tongues feel that everyone should have this gift.

4. What is the purpose of the gifts? 1 Corinthians 12:7; Ephesians 4:11-13
   To build up and to strengthen the church.

5. Why was the gift of tongues necessary? Matthew 28:19,20
   It was necessary because the gospel was new and it had to spread throughout the Roman Empire. And the disciples were unlearned men. The Holy Spirit then gave those guys the ability to communicate the gospel in other languages.

6. Can tongues be understood? Acts 2:1-11
   Yes, Those in attendance from different nations understood Peter in their own language.

7. How should I regard speaking in "unknown tongues?"
   1 Corinthians 14:9,14,19,27,28,33
   It is useless unless an interpreter is present. God is a God of order and not confusion.

8. To whom should the gift of tongues be ministered unto?
   1 Corinthians 14:22
   It is for the unbeliever so they will know how to come to Christ.

9. What is the supreme evidence that a person has received the Holy Spirit into his/her life? Galatians 5:22,23; 2 Corinthian 5:17
   A changed life. This is important because those who believe in speaking in tongues feel that speaking in tongues is the supreme evidence that a person has received the Holy Spirit.

Do you understand that ALL Christians do not have the gift of tongues?

Do you understand that the gift of tongues is not the supreme evidence of having received the Holy Spirit?

How to S-t-r-e-t-c-h Your Dollar
Lesson 18

1. What is one way in which I am commanded to honor God? Malachi 3:8-10
   By returning tithes and offerings to God. We don't pay tithes and offering to God because all of our money is His. We simply return His portion back to Him.

2. What part of my income has God especially claimed as His? Leviticus 27:30,32; Proverbs 3:9
   Ten percent and that's what tithe mean. We take it off of the gross and not the net. Proverbs 3:9 not says the first fruits or what we receive first.

3. For whose support and for what work is the tithe devoted? Numbers 18:21
   For those who minister full time for the church. The pastor is paid from the tithe. The way it works in the SDA church is that all the tithe that is collected for the month is sent up to the local conference office. They send the pastor a check once a month. If the pastor has 1,000 members or 50 members, they are paid the same (other than seniority of course). Usually in other denominations, the pastor who has 1,000 members will make much more money than the pastor with 50 members. The reason is because the pastor will get paid by what is collected that day and the money, usually, does not go up to a conference office.

4. Does the New Testament approve of the same method of support for the gospel ministry? Matthew 23:23; 1 Corinthians 9:11-14
   Yes, Jesus commended the Pharisees on paying tithes. But He condemned them for not doing other important things such as having mercy and faith.

5. How much of this world's goods belong to me? Psalms 24:1; Haggai 2:8; Psalms 50:11; 1 Corinthians 6:19,20
   Nothing. We also belong to God.

6. Who gives me the power to get wealth? Deuteronomy 8:18
   God.

7. What should be my attitude and motive in returning tithes and offerings to God?
2 Corinthians 9:7; John 14:15
A cheerful and loving giver. God does not need our money. It's a blessing to us when we return a faithful tithe and offering to Him.

Do you understand why we should return tithes and offerings to God?

If you are weak, do you want God to strengthen you in this matter?

God's Last Day Church
Lesson 19

1. How many churches did Jesus say He was going to build? Matthew 16:18
   One.

2. Has God had a special people in every age? Genesis 7:1; 18:17-33; Deuteronomy 7:7; Romans 11:5
   Yes, God used various people from different eras to proclaim His message.

3. Did all the churches that Peter, Paul, and the apostles raise up **BELIEVE** the same thing? 1 Corinthians 1:10; Ephesians 4:5
   Yes, there was no division among them.

4. Of the 250-300 different denominations in the United States and the many others throughout the world, do they all **BELIEVE** the same thing?
   No, the ones in this country although most use the same Bible, there is still division among them.

5. Does God have a remnant church or last day church today? Revelation 12:17
   Yes, they must keep all Ten Commandments and have the testimony of Jesus in their belief system. The testimony of Jesus meaning they must have the gift of prophecy. If a church does not possess at least these two things, they can be good people and present Christ as Saviour, they just cannot be the remnant church. The remnant is the last part of the church Jesus started with the disciples when He was here. The remnant will possess the same belief as the original church.

6. What are some of the beliefs of the remnant church?
   a. John 3:16; Acts 4:10-12; Ephesians 2:8, 9
      Jesus and the disciples believed Jesus was the Saviour and so does the remnant church.

   b. John 14:1-3; Acts 1:9-11; Revelation 1:7
      Jesus and the disciples believed that Jesus is coming the second time and will be seen by all and so does the remnant church.

c. Genesis 2:1-3; Exodus 20:8-11; Luke 4:14-16
Jesus and the disciples believed in the seventh day Sabbath and so does the remnant church.

d. Leviticus 11:2-10; Isaiah 66:15-17; Proverbs 20:1; Acts 10:14; Ephesians 5:18
Jesus and the disciples believed that we should not eat unclean foods and refrain from wine and strong drink and so does the remnant church.

e. Genesis 2:7; Ecclesiastes 9:5, 6, 10; Job 21:30,32; John 11:14,39,43
Jesus and the disciples believed that when a person dies they do not go to heaven or hell at the time of death but they go to the grave and so does the remnant church.

f. Leviticus 27:30-32; Malachi 3:8-10; Matthew 23:23
Jesus and the disciples believed Jesus in returning tithes and offerings and so does the remnant church.

g. Isaiah 3:16-24; 1 Timothy 2:9, 10; 1 Peter 3:3, 4
Jesus and the disciples believed Jesus in modesty in dress and so does the remnant church.

h. Revelation 12:17; 19:10; 22:8, 9; Acts 2:17,18
Jesus and the disciples believed the gift of prophecy was important for the church and so does the remnant church.

Before you ask question 7, take a sheet of paper and make two columns. The first column title it "churches" and the second column title it "Ten Commandments." Then ask your student to name denominations and you write them down on the left. After they have named some and you can help out if they cannot think of denominations. Then in the right column ask the student if the denomination they named keep all Ten Commandments. Most churches do not and they eliminate themselves from being the remnant church. If they discover a couple of denominations that do keep the Ten Commandments, then you take them through the rest of the Bible beliefs (a-h) and see what happens. For example: the Jews keep the seventh day Sabbath but they don't acknowledge Jesus as the Saviour. Or Seventh-Day Baptist. Yes, they keep the Sabbath but they still eat pork and they believe their deceased grandma is in heaven (you don't have to mention the Seventh-Day Baptist but they may bring it up). Now it is time to ask question 7. Remind them, we don't think we are better than anyone; our belief system is based on the Bible.

7. Is it clear to you that the Seventh-day Adventist church fits the above beliefs for God's last day church?

Baptism
Lesson 20

1. Why was Jesus baptized, He never sinned? Matthew 3:13-17
    Jesus was baptized to be our example. And His baptism covers those people who are not able to get baptized, such as the thief on the cross, death row criminals, death bed patients, etc.

2. What is the meaning of baptism? Roman 6:1-6
    The word baptize means "to dip" or "to immerse." Baptism is a symbolic act that demonstrates what has taken place inside a person's heart. The person has accepted Jesus as their personal Lord and Saviour and is experiencing the new life. Baptism demonstrates that when the person goes down into the watery grave to bury to the old person of sin and comes up with a new life of righteousness.

3. Is there special power in the water? Galatians 3:27; 2 Corinthians 5:17
    No, there is power only in the blood of Christ.

4. How important is baptism? Mark 16:16; John 3:1-7
    Baptism is very important. It's an act of obedience.

5. Should a person be baptized without having been taught what God expects? Matthew 28:19,20; Acts 2:36-38
    No, baptism is a conscience decision to follow Jesus and Bible truth. This rules out infant baptism.

6. How long should a person wait to be baptized after having been taught? Acts 8:36-39; 22:12-16; Psalm 119:60
    Don't wait because if you do, you may lose your desire to ever get baptized.

7. Is re-baptism a teaching in the New Testament? Acts 19:1-5
    Yes, when vital truth is absent from the life. Such as the Sabbath, health laws, state of the dead, etc. In the Acts verses, those people had not heard of the Holy Spirit.

8. What should my lifestyle be after baptism? Luke 3:12-14
   Changed for the better. If you were a thief, quit. If you were fornicator, stop.

How do you feel about being baptized into the Seventh-day Adventist church?

www.ingramcontent.com/pod-product-compliance
Lightning Source LLC
Chambersburg PA
CBHW080553170426
43195CB00016B/2782